FRANCO'S
SPAIN

EUROPE SINCE 1500:

Enlightened Despotism / JOHN G. GAGLIARDO

Franco's Spain / STANLEY G PAYNE

FRANCO'S SPAIN

Stanley G Payne

UNIVERSITY OF CALIFORNIA

LONDON
ROUTLEDGE & KEGAN PAUL LTD

First published in Great Britain 1968
by Routledge & Kegan Paul Limited
Broadway House, 68-74 Carter Lane
London, E.C.4

Copyright © 1967 by Thomas Y. Crowell Company

Printed in Great Britain by
Lowe & Brydone (Printers) Ltd. London

SBN 7100 6084 x

For My Father GEORGE C PAYNE

Preface

Contemporary Spain has been the object of much commentary and frequent hostility in the United States and elsewhere, but has received surprisingly little objective study. Hence it seemed useful to publish a brief but up-to-date analysis of the country's evolution under the Franco regime for the benefit of students of twentieth-century Europe, serious-minded travelers, and those interested in contemporary affairs. Except for the introductory chapters, the book is organized in topical fashion, with separate analyses of economics, social change, cultural development and the state of the political opposition. In this way, I have tried to balance political discussion with a consideration of the changes that have taken place in the country as a whole. Economic argument is currently all the rage in Spanish political polemics, but it has been my purpose to use only verifiable statistics in attempting to measure social and economic development. Some points are obviously matters of interpretation, and in the bibliography at the end of the book may be found suggestions for further discussion of most of the more difficult or complicated questions.

The comments of Professor Juan J. Linz of Columbia University, who read a previous draft of the manuscript, have been extremely helpful. Editor James Neyland provided assistance in preparing the copy for press. Needless to say I alone am responsible for whatever shortcomings may be found.

STANLEY G PAYNE, *Los Angeles, Calif.*

vii

Contents

Introduction

The turmoils of modern Spain reached a climax in the Civil War of 1936–39, revealing the most severe political and social cleavage found in any Western country since the French Revolution. At no time under the constitutional monarchies that governed Spain in the century prior to 1931 did the country achieve genuine representative government. This was not surprising, for political representation and self-government ultimately rest on social development, economic balance, and standards of civic culture. Though Spain had made progress in these areas, the rate was slower and more uneven than in most other large Western countries.

At the beginning of the twentieth century, half of the adult Spaniards were still illiterate. The bulk of the population lacked modern economic skills. Commercial and industrial development was concentrated in the peripheral coastal areas. The central plateau and the mountainous regions of the interior lagged well behind the rest of the country, leaving a profound regional imbalance in social and economic development. Most peasants in the southern provinces owned no land at all, and even in areas where the soil was better distributed, rural living standards were still marginal. The working classes in the towns lived more poorly than in any other part of western Europe except Portugal and southern Italy. The white-collar sectors of the lower middle class were scarcely any better off. The problem was not merely one of income, but of attitudes and values. The degree of economic initiative, as shown in the rate of formation of credit associations, rural cooperatives, or new business ventures, was clearly lower than in the more advanced countries. Even among the possessors of capital, there was scant enthusiasm for new methods and investments. Businessmen were more old-fashioned and less enterprising in Spain than in other Western lands. Perhaps partly as a result, their attitude toward employees tended to be rather severe as well. The somnolent social and economic concern of the upper classes was also accompanied by a low degree of interest in civic problems.

Parliamentary government of sorts had been instituted by sectors of the middle and upper classes during the first half of the nineteenth century. Suffrage privileges were rather generous by contemporary standards, and universal male suffrage was granted in 1890, when such rights were still a novelty in most countries as underdeveloped as Spain. Not unnaturally, the bulk of the population long remained apathetic. Voting for speechmakers in Madrid aroused scant concern among illiterate peasants, who worried mostly about growing enough to feed their families. Interest and participation in politics expanded with the growth of the lower- and middle-class urban population during the second half of the century, but the brief experience of the First Republic (1873-74) made it clear that politically conscious Spaniards felt little sense of national unity as distinct from regional loyalties, class interests, or party rivalries. Under the restored monarchy (1875-1923), political control was maintained in large measure by corruption and manipulation. The absence of constructive civic response, even among much of the middle classes, tended to discourage some of the country's leading intellectuals about the viability of political liberalism in Spain.

By the early twentieth century, domestic antagonisms were

sharpened by the emergence of political and social movements based on regional and class exclusiveness. "Regional" or "local" nationalism as it developed in Catalonia and the Basque country expressed the pride and ambition of the only areas within Spain that were beginning to develop a modern industrial society. The Catalans had a distinct historical and cultural identity of their own; after the disaster of 1898 revealed the depths of Spain's inefficacy, they began to press for regional autonomy to continue their own development unhampered by "backward Spaniards," among whom many Catalans were increasingly reluctant to be numbered. A rather similar process was taking place among the Basques. The two main branches of the Spanish working-class movement—Anarcho-Syndicalist and Socialist—slowly evolved into mass organizations. The political and social structure of the country, not to speak of its economic potential, was unprepared to deal with their demands. Nor, for that matter, could the liberal and moderate political parties of the middle classes agree among themselves. Dissension over direct representation, the autonomy of local government, executive responsibility to Parliament, foreign and military policy, and social reform made the parliamentary system almost unworkable by 1923. The dictatorship of Miguel Primo de Rivera that ruled Spain for the next seven years placed a temporary lid on these problems, then collapsed, bringing the monarchy down with it.

The resultant Second Republic was established in 1931 amid a political vacuum. Most of the moderate and conservative elements—who together comprised nearly half the population—temporarily lacked organization and expression. The Anarchist extreme left rejected parliamentary government and made ready to combat the new Republic. With all these elements either abstaining or inadequately organized, the first elections were swept by the liberal middle-class Republicans and the Socialists. A coalition composed mainly of these two groups governed the country from 1931 to 1933. Led by the doctrinaire esthete Manuel

Azaña, the liberal administration separated Church and state, drastically reduced the Army officer corps, granted regional autonomy to Catalonia, and established arbitration committees for economic disputes. Though this did not at all satisfy the extreme left, it was more than most moderates had bargained for. Anti-clerical legislation shocked Spain's large Catholic population, encouraging formation of a clerical party, known from its initials as the CEDA. This group stood for basic constitutional reforms to achieve a corporative system that would protect Catholic privileges. By 1933, the Socialist-Republican coalition broke down over economic issues, and new elections were called. Though the Spanish voting system favored coalition tickets, the middle-class Republican liberals and Socialists both ran independently, whereas the CEDA formed a broad coalition with other moderate and conservative parties. The enfranchisement of women, who were politically more conservative, was another advantage for the center-rightist coalition, which won a lopsided victory in the 1933 elections.

During the next three years, Spanish affairs were strongly influenced by developments abroad. Leftist leaders were frightened by the Nazi triumph in Germany (1933) and the *coup d'état* by which clerical fascists took over Austria (1934). The fate of the Italian working class movement under Mussolini was obvious, and the feeling grew that "fascism" was also a threat in Spain. Actually, there were very few "fascists" in the country in 1933–34, for the only genuinely fascistic movement, the Falange, had only a few thousand members. To leftists, however, the fact that the CEDA had won a plurality of seats in the recent election was ominous enough. The main group of Socialist activists repented collaboration with the Republicans, for the agrarian reform had scarcely even begun and the depression crisis was deepening, while trade union leaders were not satisfied with the mild reforms of middle-class liberals. Though the new administration in 1934 was organized by moderates,

CEDA leaders pressed for cabinet posts and talked of rewriting the constitution. A Catalan law to protect Catalan tenant farmers and sharecroppers was vetoed by the Spanish Supreme Court, supported by the central government. It was only a matter of time before several CEDA ministers would be brought into the cabinet, and Socialists and Catalan Nationalists prepared for rebellion to prevent the Spanish Republic from "going fascist."

The revolt of October 1934 was put down by the Army, but not before Socialists and Anarchists had proclaimed social revolution in the northwestern mining province of Asturias and at least one thousand people had been killed. The rebellion sharply polarized political opinion. Many middle-class moderates who had heretofore voted for the center began to come down on the side of the Right in order, as they saw it, to conserve their lives and property. The repression of the Left and the suspension of Catalan autonomy was carried out with such vindictiveness that the opposition became more alienated than ever. Yet the conservatives were unable to capitalize on the defeat of the revolutionaries. They lacked an absolute parliamentary majority and had to cooperate with their allies in the center parties who, thanks to the scruples of the President of the Republic, held most of the cabinet posts.

The next elections, in February 1936, were contested by a Popular Front of Republican liberals, Socialists, Catalanists, and Communists (supported by the Anarchists) and a National Front of clericals, conservatives, and monarchists. The Popular Front program pledged return to the original Republican policy of 1931–32 but espoused no radical changes. National Front spokesmen postulated constitutional reforms to achieve a corporative system of government. The Popular Front, supported by most of the lower classes and part of the middle classes, got from 50 to 52 percent of the popular vote; its rival, supported by most of the middle classes, received between 42 and 45 percent, but the actual distribution of seats gave the Popular Front a majority of nearly two to one in the new Parliament. The center parties were almost wiped out.

After the elections were over, the Socialists, who had the second largest individual group of deputies in the new Parliament, refused to continue the Popular Front alliance with the liberals. A government was formed entirely of middle-class Republican liberals, but the latter had only 121 out of 473 seats, and a stable majority was nowhere to be found. The self-proclaimed goal of the Anarchists and majority Socialists was violent class revolution; and, during the spring and early summer of 1936, the economy was plagued by conflicts of almost every description. Most radical of all were the landless peasants of the south, heretofore largely ignored by political leaders. After the Popular Front victory, encouraged by Socialist and Anarchist propaganda, they believed their hour had arrived. During March and April, 1936, they occupied thousands of acres of property, mostly belonging to absentee landlords. To conservative property owners, this was social revolution on the march.

Ever since the beginning of the Republic, a small clique of monarchists had plotted its overthrow. This element was largely responsible for an abortive Army revolt in 1932. By 1936, the small Falangist group of outright fascists added to the tension by its numerous street fights with leftists. For several years, both monarchists and Falangists had been inciting Army leaders to rebel, but with scant success. By the spring of 1936, some of the more active, politically conservative Army leaders began to plan direct action of their own.

During the months of June and July, 1936, the situation was highly confused. Despite all their talk of violent revolution, despite all the strikes and street fights, the Anarchists and majority Socialists had no concrete plan for revolution or for taking over the government. There is some evidence that, by the end of June, the radical faction within the Socialists was beginning to lose its influence. By this time, however, a great many moderates and conservatives had given up hope of being able to deal with the liberal Republican government. The Republican chief, Azaña, now President, was bitterly disillusioned and lacked the will to impose his leadership. The administration refused to take strong measures against extremists on either side, arguing that it was better to let them burn themselves out rather than inflaming matters further. But it was not the extremists who were burnt out first.

The social, political, and religious issues that divided Spaniards in 1936 need not of themselves have issued into full-scale civil war. However, the organs of mediation and conciliation had completely broken down, and the politically active minority was mostly dominated by doctrinaire, rigid groups that rejected practical compromise as a political technique. Socialists, Anarchists, Communists, monarchists, Falangists, clerical authoritarians, and military activists all wanted a sharp break with the existing situation rather than a constructive agreement that might assuage tensions.

The spark that finally set off the war was the murder of the leader of the monarchists by insubordinate members of the Republican security forces. Though the guilty were suspended and placed under arrest, the symbolic implications of this deed threw many undecided moderates and conservatives on the side of anti-Republican extremists. Five days later, on July 17, 1936, portions of the Army rose in revolt against the liberal Republican government; and, within seventy-two hours, most of Spain was divided between two warring camps.

1 / Francisco Franco

The Army rebellion that spearheaded the reaction of middle-class Spaniards against the challenge of the Popular Front began without clear leadership or organization. Within less than three months, however, the most famous general in the Spanish Army, Francisco Franco, emerged as rebel Commander-in-chief and Chief of State. Paradoxically, until the final year or so before the Civil War, Franco had not been a typical Spanish "political general," but had seemed a model of professionalism who steered clear of politics.

Franco was born on December 4, 1892, at the naval center of El Ferrol on the northwestern coast of Spain. His family had a tradition of naval service and, though it could trace a few minor connections with the petty nobility, in fact belonged to the bureaucratic strata of the Spanish middle classes. Franco's father was an officer in the naval supply system. His salary was slight, but the family had no other source of income and lived in strait circumstances, made the more stringent by the irresponsible personal habits of its head. The elder Franco seems to have been an emotional rebel against middle-class conventions and something of a scandal in local society because of his drinking and skirtchasing. The five children were reared by their pious, long-suffering mother, who tried to instill in them her own sense of religion, discipline, and duty. The youngest brother, Ramón, clearly identified with his father. After he grew up, he became an Air Force officer, piloted the first trans-Atlantic flight to Argentina, led a daredevil personal and professional life, and for long was associated with the extreme left in politics, organizing a military revolt against the monarchy in 1930. Francisco, on the other hand, seems to have been influenced much more by his mother. The scant evidence indicates that his childhood years were unhappy and that he was personally sensitive about his father's reputation. Certainly he never emulated the latter's habits.

Franco hoped to follow family tradition by becoming a naval officer, but could not gain entrance to the Naval Academy and was enrolled in the Army's Infantry Academy at Toledo, instead. Franco was at least a full year younger than most officer candidates when he began his studies. After graduating with the rest of his class in 1910, he was commissioned second lieutenant while still less than 18 years of age. Garrison duty in the Spanish Army of the early twentieth century was a boring, stultifying, largely futile existence. For a shy, introverted, socially maladroit teenaged lieutenant, it had few attractions; and therefore in 1912, Franco volunteered for active service in the only area where the Spanish Army was engaged in combat, northern Morocco. During the next year, treaties were signed establishing a Spanish Protectorate over the northern 5 percent of the former Moroccan empire. The local tribes were unruly and warlike, while Spanish diplomacy was crude and ineffective. The occupation of Spanish Morocco soon became a military problem. To reduce Spanish losses and spearhead the military activities, elite units of Moorish police and "Regular" troops were formed. Their leaders were volunteers from the Spanish officer corps, who earned prestige, combat experience, and higher pay. One of the first junior officers to volunteer to command a platoon of Moorish *Regulares* was Francisco Franco.

At no time does Franco seem to have been popular with his fellow officers. Even at the age of twenty, he was withdrawn, with very few friends, uninterested in the social diversions, the drinking, gambling, and whoring that filled the leisure of most officers in Morocco. Franco had never been used to having a good time. Life to him was hard and serious, requiring strict attention and discipline. Unlike most of his colleagues, he spent evenings in his tent going over maps and supply lists. Though never familiar with his men, he tried to look after their needs and provide strict supervision of problems. He maintained rigorous discipline, which was submitted to more readily because of Franco's personal example in combat. Though not reckless, he was known never to shirk positions of danger but to advance at the head of his troops often in an almost mechanical, fatalistic fashion. This combination of qualities made him stand out among the brave, but sloppy and ineffective, Spanish officers in Morocco. He was quickly promoted to first lieutenant and then to captain at the age of twenty-two. Casualties among the *Regulares'* officers were the highest of any section of the Army, and it seemed only a matter of time until odds would catch up with him. During a small engagement in 1916, he was felled by a bullet in the abdomen. Though it was a serious wound, he managed to recover and was promoted to major at the age of twenty-three.

After four years of combat duty, Franco was assigned to the infantry brigade in the Oviedo garrison in Asturias. He became known as the *comandantín* ("little major"), not altogether because his short stature of five feet three inches was so unusual among Spanish officers, but because of his extreme youth as well. Franco was apparently discontented and ill-at-ease at Oviedo, for the polite society of a provincial capital made him uncomfortable, and the only activity in which he had really felt adequate—combat—was not to be had. He applied for admission to the Army's Staff College for further training but was told that officers of such senior rank—even if only twenty-three years old —were not admitted. The way out finally came in 1920 with the organization of a special volunteer "Legion," based on the French Foreign Legion, for service in Spanish Morocco. Franco immediately volunteered and was named commander of the Legion's First Battalion. After the total collapse of the forces in the eastern part of the Protectorate in 1921, the Legion was mainly responsible for defending the bridgehead around Melilla and starting the counteroffensive against the Moroccan rebels of Abd el Krim. After the Legion's commander was killed in combat in 1923, Franco was named to replace him and promoted to lieutenant colonel, and not long afterward to full colonel. At the age of thirty, he had become head of the elite section of the Spanish Army. The Legion continued to play a major role in the final campaigns to pacify the Protectorate under Primo de Rivera in 1924–27. When it was over, Franco was a thirty-three-year-old brigadier, one of the youngest generals in Europe, the most famous of the younger officers in the Army, and renowned for personal courage, combat direction, professional discipline, and qualities of leadership.

In 1923, he had married Carmen Polo, the pretty, seventeen-year-old daughter of a wealthy Asturian businessman, finally overcoming the solitude of his barren private life. Maturity brought Franco greater ease in social intercourse, and during the next years he demonstrated an animation in personal relations and a loquacity in discourse that contrasted somewhat with his comportment in both the early and later periods of his career. Franco's private life soon was ordered exclusively by his wife, who arranged a not atypical upper middle-class household with a strong dose of formal Catholic piety. This, in itself, was something of a change for Franco, who in his early years in Morocco seemed to have little regard for religion.

In 1928, the Primo de Rivera dictatorship established a General Military Academy in Zaragoza to provide officer candidates a firm grounding in military psychology and *esprit de corps*. Franco, as the epitome of the rigid attitude of the Moroccan veterans, was named its Director. Lacking advanced technical and theoretical training, he found it difficult to handle the more complicated details of military pedagogy, but assembled a competent teaching staff to cope with the problems. Some of the officers who taught under Franco in the years 1928–31 held high rank in the Spanish Army after 1936. At the beginning of his new duties, Franco made his first and only trip outside the Spanish world, undertaking a brief tour of German military schools.

He played no role in the political turmoil of 1930–31, though other officers figured prominently in the resignation of Primo de Rivera, the makeshift royal ministries that followed, and the conspiracies that helped precipitate collapse of the monarchy. The only political initiative Franco had ever shown was his opposition to what had appeared to be Primo de Rivera's "defeatism" in Morocco in 1924. Yet he never translated that hostility into action, but remained a loyal subordinate who was amply rewarded. In the last years of the monarchy, Franco's prominence in the Army was recognized by appointment as one of the king's "Lords of the Bedchamber," a signal honor of which he was apparently quite proud. Franco was mortified by the highly publicized activities of his younger brother Ramón in leading an Air Force conspiracy against the monarchy, and he did almost everything possible to underline his own loyalty to the regime. Ramón subsequently published several letters from Francisco where the latter begged him to cease bringing opprobrium on the family name.

Like most of the Army hierarchy, Franco stood by rather helplessly and confused as the monarchy collapsed and the Second Republic was proclaimed. Though known for his obedience to the monarchy, he made no hostile gesture against the new regime. However, the key Republican liberal, Azaña, who became Minister of War, was determined to carry out a drastic reorganization of the Army to remove one of the mainstays of the old order. A liberal retirement system induced over half the officers to terminate their military careers. The unit system was drastically revised, and an effort was made to "democratize" the officer corps. The General Academy at Zaragoza was closed because it was deemed too caste-minded, and all the campaign merits awarded by the late Dictator were canceled, dropping Franco from the top to the bottom of the seniority list at the rank of brigadier.

The Azaña reforms were a grievous personal and professional disappointment to Franco, but he had little choice other than to accept them. The liberal Republican star was in the ascendant in 1931, and Franco was careful not to offend the new regime by overt word or deed. Though he was left without assignment for nearly a year, his tacit submission was rewarded in 1932 when he was given command of the infantry garrison at La Coruña. He carefully dissociated himself from the rebellion of a handful of ranking officers against the government in August of that year, correctly calculating that the liberals were still firmly in control. His circumspection received its due in 1933 when he was transferred to the more important post of garrison commander in the Balearic Islands.

After the liberals fell from power, the Centrist government of 1934 adopted a more conciliatory approach to the Army. One indication of this was Franco's promotion to major general, once again the youngest in the Spanish Army. His work impressed the current War Minister, who had Franco invited to Madrid as temporary technical advisor to the General Staff during the late summer field exercises. He was still in the capital when the leftist revolt broke out in Asturias. Franco's services were retained by the General Staff, where he played a major role in organizing the repression of the rebels. During the following year, the political pendulum swung to the Right, strongly favoring Franco. He had always been politically identified with conservative nationalism; moreover, his sister-in-law's husband, Ramón Serrano Súñer, was leader of the youth movement of the CEDA, the main conservative coalition. In 1935, Franco became closely identified with the CEDA. He was named Commander-in-chief of the elite forces stationed in Morocco; then, after the CEDA head José María Gil Robles became War Minister in May, he was appointed Chief of the General Staff.

During the nine months that he directed the General Staff, Franco endeavored both to raise the Army's combat efficiency and to guarantee the dominance of conservative, anti-leftist officers, reversing the direction of the Azaña reforms. There were frequent rumors in 1935 that Gil Robles was going to use the War Ministry for a *coup d'état* that would impose an authoritarian, corporatist regime on Spain. He persistently denied this gossip, and there is no indication that Franco himself was involved in any machinations to take over the government. After the center-rightist coalition broke down in late autumn, forcing Gil Robles to resign the War Ministry, the CEDA chief investigated the possibility of resisting this by force, but Franco said that the Army was "morally disunited" and that forceful intervention in public affairs might very likely precipitate disaster.

On the night of February 16, 1936, after it was becoming clear that the Popular Front had won the new election, the major rightist leaders urged Franco and the interim Minister of War to declare martial law, annulling the leftist victory. Though sorely disappointed and apprehensive about the future, Franco still refused to intervene on his own initiative. The disasters of Army politics under Primo de Rivera were fresh in his mind; and, despite the urging of a minority of military radicals, the Army commanders stood by while the new Azaña government was formed.

The return of the liberals marked another reversal of military policy. Franco was removed as Chief of Staff and banished to a kind of gilded exile as commander of the small garrison of the island of Tenerife, hundreds of miles away in the Canaries. Similarly, the key appointments made during the previous year were changed, nominees of Franco and Gil Robles being replaced by more liberal officers. A number of the conservative and/or nationalist leaders in the Army held a meeting in Madrid in mid-March to discuss their course of action. There is evidence that Franco advised moderation at this point, suggesting that Azaña, for all his inadequacies, was not a radical leftist, and if given time would perhaps be able to work things out.

But things worked out badly in the spring of 1936. Azaña was unable to control the extremes of either Left or Right and eventually gave up trying. On a dubious technicality, the Popular Front majority deposed Alcalá Zamora, the moderate Republican President, and elected Azaña in his place. This relieved Azaña of immediate executive responsibility, while the removal of a genuinely middle-of-the-road President had the more serious effect of eliminating one of the last potential guarantees against leftist subversion. While the climate of violence thickened, efforts were made to develop a broadly based military conspiracy. Nominal leader was General José Sanjurjo, in Lisbon exile, but the real co-ordinator was Brigadier Emilio Mola, commander of the Pamplona garrison in the northeast. Many officers supported the plot, though with complete diversity of views and objectives. Some conspirators were monarchists, some were fascists, and a few were clerical reactionaries, but the majority were ordinary middle-class officers without elaborate ideological designs who simply wanted to avoid chaos or a leftist takeover. Since the recent changes, however, most of the senior officers in command were loyal supporters of the regime. This fact, as well as the extreme diversity of views among the rebels and the hesitation even of many anti-Popular Front officers, placed the conspiracy in great difficulty.

Mola and most of the other leading plotters deemed it most

important to have Franco's support because of his reputation, experience, and following in the Army. Though he had few personal friends, he was almost universally respected and was very influential among the vital elite units in Morocco, the only well-equipped, well-trained, combatworthy sectors of the Army. But if the conspirators were strongly interested in Franco, he was lukewarm about the conspiracy. He knew the officer corps was confused and divided and had no wish to ruin an illustrious career through one rash stroke. His prudence in 1931–32 had paid off, and another spin of the wheel of political fortune might change things again. Even as a combat officer in Morocco, Franco had never been merely reckless. As he grew older and began to face major responsibilities, his tendency toward calculation and outright delay became more pronounced. He promised fellow officers that he would "do his duty," but refused to commit himself concretely to the conspiracy. On June 25, 1936, he wrote a letter to President Azaña warning that the government's present policy toward the Army might ultimately erode its morale and loyalty. There is no indication of a reply.

Franco apparently did not cast his lot with the conspirators until after the first of July. What finally convinced him to take this step is partly a matter of conjecture. Having little or no understanding of social or economic problems, he could scarcely fathom Spain's basic difficulties, but he was keenly aware of public disorder and mass leftist revolutionary organizations. He apparently decided that the situation within Spain had become so precarious that it would be more dangerous to sit back and watch matters slide than to join the rebels. His allegiance was not given without condition, for he insisted on taking command of the elite Army of Morocco during the revolt. This was readily agreed to because of his great influence among those vital units.

On July 18–19, 1936, Franco was flown by private airplane from the Canary Islands to Tetuán, capital of the Spanish Protectorate in Morocco, where, within the past twenty-four hours, the Army had rebelled and seized power from the government authorities. The same thing happened in approximately one-third of the home provinces of Spain, but the rebel Army units that came out in revolt were too weak to handle the loyal security forces of the Popular Front regime and the tens of thousands of leftist militia that were being armed. Success of the military rebellion depended almost entirely on transporting the 32,000-man force in Morocco across the straits to seize the capital before the reorganized left-liberal government could consolidate its position and crush the rebels in northern Spain. Yet the rebellion in the Navy was a failure, and a sizable Popular Front fleet established a blockade of the north Moroccan coast.

Within forty-eight hours of taking command in Spanish Morocco, Franco was faced with an absolute crisis. Unless he could find means to move the bulk of his shock forces to the Spanish mainland, the rebellion would very possibly collapse within a matter of weeks. By July 21, Franco decided to seek assistance abroad as the only means of averting potential catastrophe. The liberal parliamentary states would probably be hostile to the rebellion against the Spanish Popular Front regime, whereas German and Italian agents had already indicated that the fascist powers of Central Europe would take a more friendly attitude. Through the German consul in Lisbon, Franco requested a squadron of transport planes to move part of his troops to Spain. Seeing that this would draw no quick response, on the following day he dispatched a small group of personal representatives to Berlin by air. At the same time, both Franco and Mola, commander of the rebel forces in northern Spain, sent missions to Rome to request aerial and other assistance from the Italian regime. Conservative diplomats in the two fascist countries resisted involvement in the confused, uncertain Spanish situation, but it was not difficult to convince Hitler and high Nazi leaders that the Spanish military rebellion was struggling to create a bulwark against "Communism" and "liberal decadence."

An authoritarian rightist regime in southwestern Europe might be associated profitably with the foreign policies of both Hitler and Mussolini. The German decision to assist the rebels was made on July 26; that of the Italian regime came on the following day.

Before the end of July, the first German and Italian bombing and transport planes began to arrive in Spanish Morocco, initiating the first major airlift of troops and materiél in modern military history. During the next two months, nearly 20,000 troops and a great deal of materiél were flown across the straits, while the assistance of Italian bombers eventually helped to break the Republican naval blockade. During the first week in August, the shock troops from the Protectorate began a long march northward against Madrid. In a series of rapid moves, all southwestern Spain was occupied within six weeks. The Popular Front regime had to rely on workers' militia that lacked discipline, leadership, and training. Though greatly superior in numbers to Franco's small professional units, they were helpless in the field and were routed time and again. By the end of September, Franco's spearheads were only forty miles from Madrid, which was being prepared by the leftist groups for last-ditch resistance.

During the first weeks, the military situation had been so precarious that the rebel leaders had little time to think about the political goals they were fighting for. As indicated, the diversity of political criteria among the Army insurgents and their civilian auxiliaries was extreme. Nominal leader of the rebel junta was to have been General Sanjurjo, but he was killed in an airplane accident when attempting to fly from Lisbon to rebel headquarters. For the time being, Mola established a "National Defense Junta" in Burgos under the titular direction of Miguel Cabanellas, the Army's oldest general on active duty. Franco, as commander of the vital Army of the South, was included as the junta's ninth member on August 3.

Initially, about the only point that Insurgent officers agreed upon was that they had rebelled, as they put it, to "save Spain." For whom or from what was not always clearly defined. The only unifying note of rebel propaganda was a broad appeal to Spanish nationalism, as opposed to international Communist subversion or so-called "dissolvent influences." The two most active auxiliary groups behind the rising were the Falangists and the ultra-clerical Carlist traditionalists; but, as a broad generalization, it might be said that the bulk of the Spanish middle classes rallied to the insurgents within a few weeks. It was soon discovered that one of the most effective devices for generating support among the more conservative sectors was a broad appeal to Catholicism. Though Mola had originally planned to maintain the Republic's separation of Church and state, Catholic opinion, except in Catalonia and the Basque country, rallied to the rebels almost one hundred percent. All the while, little or nothing was said about the ultimate kind of government the insurgents were fighting for, other than that it would be based on nationalism, Catholicism, order, and social justice. Though monarchists had been very active in promoting the rebel "Nationalist" movement, insurgent generals were careful to avoid direct mention of royalism, understanding that monarchist feeling had very little backing among the Spanish people as a whole.

By September, when Franco's field columns were preparing for the final drive toward Madrid, several influential personalities in the rebel camp decided that the time had come to broach the question of political leadership. With the decisive phase of the conflict approaching, opinion in the Army was widespread that a *mando único*—unified command under a single leader—should be established to guarantee coordinated direction in the final struggle. The monarchist politicians, who were proving very helpful as diplomatic agents and who had a number of supporters in the rebel command, wanted to see firm direction established by a reliable conservative general who could be trusted

to restore the monarchy as soon as possible. It was clearly understood that the elderly Cabanellas, a Mason and a moderate
liberal, was a mere figurehead who had been appointed to encourage military unity and rally the lukewarm. Meanwhile, the
German and Italian representatives at Lisbon were urging the
Nationalists to form a regular government as soon as possible, so
as to win greater recognition and support.

The initiative was taken by General Alfredo Kindelán, a
staunch monarchist and commander of the small Nationalist air
force. He arranged a meeting of the Burgos Junta near Salamanca on September 21 to discuss establishment of a *mando
único*. At the conference, all the senior rebel officers supported
the idea except Cabanellas, whose actual influence was very
slight. Kindelán then advanced the name of Franco as Commander-in-chief. There is no evidence that anyone demurred,
for the choice seemed fully logical. Francisco Franco was the
most famous, and perhaps the most respected, general in the
Army. No one could equal his combat record or rally similar
support among the elite units that were doing the most important fighting. Franco commanded the key sector of the Nationalist forces and was more highly esteemed in Germany and Italy
than any other insurgent general. Moreover, he had until recently kept out of politics and was not associated with authoritarian reactionary elements to the extent that some of his more
important colleagues were. Even Mola, his only possible rival,
recognized the force of these arguments. Franco's recognition
as Generalissimo was apparently agreed upon without a single
dissenting vote.

During the week that followed, however, Cabanellas made
no move in Burgos to issue the proclamation of Franco's command, and the latter's backers became worried. Chief among
them was the General's brother, Nicolás, currently serving as
the insurgents' representative in Lisbon. Nicolás seems to have
found it hard to convince Franco that he should actually take the

lead in asserting his authority, for the latter remembered the failure of Primo de Rivera's attempt at dictatorship and was reluctant to press things too far. At this juncture, Nicolás summoned the services of Lt. Col. Juan Yagüe, key commander of the Spanish Legion and until recently head of the field columns operating outside Madrid. Yagüe was a Falangist and a fervent Nationalist who wanted the rebels to establish a dictatorship that could undertake sweeping reforms. On the evening of September 27, he made a speech outside Franco's headquarters in Cáceres where he stressed that the shock units demanded elevation of Franco as *jefe único*. On the following day, Yagüe accompanied Franco and Kindelán to a second conference with the junta members. Kindelán read a decree he had prepared, naming Franco not merely *generalísimo* of the armed forces but also "chief of government" who would "assume all the powers of the state"—in other words, Nationalist dictator. Some of the junta members were taken aback, for this had gone beyond what they had planned. Yagüe later claimed that he had threatened to lead a revolt of the shock units unless the decree were promulgated. By this time, the insurgent generals had gone too far to back down, and they accepted the *fait accompli* arranged by Franco's backers. On October 1, 1936, he was proclaimed Chief of the Nationalist State.

If Franco had demonstrated considerable diffidence and uncertainty in moving toward the command of the rebel movement, he exhibited no doubts after becoming Dictator. After all, he had done very little to gain such power. The conspirators had done everything possible to coax him to join the rebellion; and, with only a certain amount of encouragement, a group of personal supporters had elevated him to absolute power. Afterward he apparently felt that the hand of divine destiny lay upon him, that God had chosen him to lead Spain. The religious influence of his pious wife, increasing age, and the adulation of religious leaders and political sycophants all helped to build this attitude.

Yet even Franco's strongest supporters scarcely imagined in 1936 the duration of the regime that was being created. The General's backers had pressed his personal rule to facilitate victory in the final battle of the Civil War and to assure the transition to a more permanent conservative and authoritarian regime, preferably a restored monarchy. What upset the calculations of most rebel leaders was the stout resistance of Madrid in November, 1936. The Civil War did not end that autumn, but continued for nearly two and one-half years. In the process, the Generalissimo thoroughly consolidated his personal power.

2 / Politics and Diplomacy of the Franco Regime

The Spanish rebels' planning had been based throughout on the hope of a quick military decision. In the early autumn of 1936, when Franco became head of the insurgent forces, every indication pointed toward a speedy conclusion to the conflict. With the Republican regime denied the accepted right under international law of a recognized government to purchase arms to defend itself from rebellion, the military situation of the Popular Front militia was indeed critical.

Changing international pressures had already proved decisive in the evolution of the Spanish struggle, just as they had influenced the radicalization of the country's political environment in the years preceding. Creation of the so-called "Non-Intervention Committee" by Great Britain and France to discourage association of other powers with the warring forces in Spain might soon have sealed the fate of the Popular Front regime, had not the Soviet Union decided by the end of the summer to intervene on behalf of the latter. Already preoccupied by the extension of fascist power in Central Europe, Stalin con-

16

cluded that it was not desirable to see a right-wing dictatorship established in Spain without countervailing leftist pressure. The arrival of the first shipments of Russian materiél and Communist-organized volunteers in October-November 1936 was of great importance in stiffening the Popular Front's defense of Madrid. Franco's victorious columns were stopped when within only a few kilometers of their final objective.

Heretofore, the rebels had relied primarily on a small number of elite, semi-professional units. Trained reserves were few and stockpiles of materiél, non-existent. The "Nationalists" were placed at a serious numerical disadvantage by the large numbers of enthusiastic, if untrained and undisciplined, Popular Front volunteers. If the great majority of fervent Catholics supported the rebels, religion had lost its influence among large sectors of the population. Public opinion mostly supported the Popular Front regime except in the more conservative rural provinces, and time seemed to work against the rebels.

It was not possible for Franco to generate the military and economic strength within the Nationalist zone to overcome the Popular Front coalition. By the end of 1936, nearly half of Spain was in the hands of the insurgents, but this included almost none of the industrial regions. Time would be needed to build a mass army, and the technical and economic assistance for such an effort in large measure would have to come from outside Spain. Fortunately for Franco, the German and Italian governments were ready and willing. On November 18, 1936, they officially recognized the rebel regime as the legal government of Spain. An entire German air corps, the "Condor Legion" of approximately 100 combat planes, had already been dispatched to Spain, and military equipment flowed steadily.

Mussolini proved equally helpful, conceiving the notion of an "Italian crusade against Bolshevism" in the West Mediterranean. This would bolster the military and diplomatic interests of his regime and enhance the martial image of Italian Fascism.

During 1937–38, Italy provided much of the equipment with which the Nationalist forces operated. After Franco's failure to take Madrid in a series of flanking maneuvers during the winter of 1936–37, the rebel shock units were near exhaustion, and Mussolini decided to boost them to victory by dispatching a large combat group of Italian "volunteers." The resulting "Corpo di Truppe Volontarie," which arrived in Spain during the first months of 1937, amounted to some 25,000 combat troops, organized in three divisions and two extra brigades. Some of the soldiers were regular army men, but many were from the Black Shirt militia and lacked proper training or leadership. The result was the famous check of an Italian attack near Guadalajara by Republican forces in March 1937. After this frustration, Franco gave up plans for another direct assault on Madrid. During the spring of 1937, the main Nationalist effort was devoted to sealing off and occupying the Basque region in the north. In June, while flying to headquarters to report on these operations, the organizer of the rebellion, General Emilio Mola, was killed in a plane crash.

During the winter and spring of 1937, the Nationalist command pressed efforts to develop a mass Army. Limited conscription was begun in the rebel zone in the first weeks of the war and had become general by the close of 1937. To provide leadership, a series of officer-training schools was created with German assistance. Its candidates were chosen from among young men of the middle classes who possessed some degree of education and were eager to fight against the revolution that had occurred in the Popular Front zone. By the end of the war, these schools had produced 25,000 second lieutenants and almost as many sergeants, or the bulk of the officer corps of the new Nationalist Army. Thanks to German instruction and the large nucleus of professional officers with which the rebels had begun, they were able to retain throughout the war a greater degree of cohesion than was ever developed among the semi-amateur units of the Republican Army. By the late spring of 1937, the Nationalist forces for the first time approached numerical parity with the Republicans, each side having more than 350,000 men under arms.

While the Nationalist Army developed its manpower and leadership cadres, Franco had to insure the large amounts of materiél that would be necessary to achieve victory. Mussolini was no problem; for, after his prestige had been committed, he felt that he must see Franco through to victory or suffer a severe personal defeat. Though the Nationalist regime was unable temporarily to pay for more than a very small portion of the massive shipments of Italian arms, almost unlimited credit was extended.

The German government was more difficult. Hitler had been careful never to identify himself as closely with the Nationalist cause as had Mussolini. He preferred to use the Spanish struggle to tie down the attention of the Western democracies and to keep the Soviet Union committed, giving Germany greater latitude for her rearmament and political machinations in Central Europe. In November 1937, he went so far as to tell German officials that a quick victory for Franco was not desirable, for that would remove the Spanish conflict from the spotlight and make it easier for other powers to focus on Central Europe.

Though the German regime also extended broad credit to the Nationalists, it demanded something in return. Exports of Spanish minerals to Germany increased greatly in 1937, and Franco finally conceded an adjustment of Spanish regulations on foreign investment, making it possible for the German government trading company in Spain to convert some of the credit from arms shipment to purchase up to 40 percent of the stock in several mining interests. Though the extent of German and Italian influence in Nationalist Spain provoked murmuring even among ardent pro-Franco elements, Franco kept it strictly limited to military and economic affairs, retaining full political power. In the process, he guaranteed continuation of the German and Italian arms shipments until final victory had been won.

Having little political experience or imagination, and under heavy pressures of military command, Franco long delayed formal organization of his government. For the first sixteen months, he perpetuated the system of military supervision hastily slapped together by Mola at the beginning of the conflict. Much of the responsibility for the initial political structure of the regime rested on Franco's brother-in-law, Ramón Serrano Súñer, who escaped from a Republican jail and made his way to the rebel zone early in 1937. In the three years before the Civil War, Serrano had provided Franco's main political contacts. The General was accustomed to listening to his brother-in-law's advice and quickly installed the ex-CEDA youth leader as chief counsellor. The German and Italian governments were both pressing Franco to do something to create a regular political structure, for this would strengthen his diplomatic position among the major powers—most of whom had not recognized his government —and would make it easier to rally support among the Spanish people, a great many of whom did not favor the insurgent regime.

There were few elements on which to build, for the principal conservative groupings had been swept away by the outbreak of the Civil War. The main civilian auxiliaries of the rebels came from the fascistic Falange and the reactionary, clerical Carlists. The latter, who championed the return of a traditionalist monarchy, enjoyed popular support only in the province of Navarre and a few other scattered districts. The Falangists had little following before the elections of 1936; but, under threat of Civil War, tens of thousands of people joined to give Falangism a sizable following. The Falangist doctrines of imperialism, violence, national unity under dictatorship, and a corporative system of national syndicates (trade unions) to control social and economic problems seemed ready-made for a self-styled Nationalist regime struggling with the challenge of total civil war. It also reflected the dominant fascistic trend in Central and western Europe during these years. Moreover, from the regime's point of view, there was the added advantage that the Falangists had lost nearly all their original leaders in the first months of the Civil War. The movement's followers were an amorphous mass, without strong ideological direction and without a head.

After hasty planning by Serrano, in April 1937, Franco declared the establishment of a reorganized "Falange Española Tradicionalista," fusing Carlists with Falangists as the official political movement of the Nationalist state. The original Falangist doctrines of imperialism, violence, nationalist dictatorship, and national syndicalism were adopted as the ideology of the government. This orientation also included certain notions of anti-capitalism and, as far as many Falangists were concerned, of non-clericalism, with some emphasis on social reform. It was partly counterbalanced by the influence of ultra-conservative, clerical, and monarchist intellectuals of the Acción Española group, whose own principles were a Spanish version of the ideology of the Action Française. Thus the regime acquired a fascistic façade in many ways roughly comparable with that of Germany and Italy, though its strong stress on Catholicism was more reminiscent of the minor authoritarian states of Portugal and Austria. However, contrary to leftist opinion, Franco was not driven to this move by Hitler and Mussolini. Rather, he made it on the advice of Serrano as the only logical way of achieving an ideological and political platform for his Nationalist military dictatorship.

In his first proclamation, the Generalissimo made it clear that he was not handing power to the Falange but taking over the Falange for the purposes of his government. The new "FET" was not conceived as a narrow doctrinaire group, but as a Nationalist unitary party for all the followers of the regime, be they fascists, clericals, monarchists, conservatives, or even moderate liberals. Even the program of the new Falange, he said, was subject to change as the needs of Nationalist Spain shifted. Though Franco was fond of dwelling on the adjective "totalitarian" in referring to the political structure of his government, he emphasized that this was not derived from the standards of Nazism and Italian Fascism so much as from the Spanish past, from the first "national monarchy" of Ferdinand and Isabella, which had achieved a high degree of central control, had conquered Moors, expelled Jews, and burnt heretics at the stake. Spanish "fascism" or "integral nationalism" would, in short, be based on the intolerant, ultra-Catholic norms of Spanish history —on the policies that had resulted in the so-called "Black Legend" of Spanish government and society.

Franco's first regular cabinet was not named until January 30, 1938. It was eclectic in the extreme, consisting of two monarchists, two Carlists, two Falangists, two personal supporters without other allegiance, and two non-aligned generals. Altogether, four of the ten cabinet members were from the military, underlining the fact that the Army remained the ultimate basis of the dictatorship. The military hierarchy supported Franco, provided he continued to play fair with them and defer to their wishes in important matters. The monarchists had encouraged creation of the dictatorship to facilitate transition to a monarchy, but the continuation of a desperate Civil War postponed all their plans indefinitely. Though establishment of the FET made the restoration of the monarchy seem even more remote, they had no alternative but to back Franco all the way.

Internal security, which had been a problem from the beginning, was maintained through wholesale terrorism. Since mass executions of political enemies were carried out on both sides of the barricades in the first days of the Civil War, it is not possible to show that one side was more responsible than the other for "starting it." However, the Popular Front forces never conquered new territory during the Civil War and so never gained control of new political enemies to purge. After the first six months, most of the obvious foes had been slaughtered in the Republican zone; and, by that time, the anarchic elements in the Popular Front were being brought under control, putting an end to 90 percent of the "Red" killings. The Nationalists, on the other hand, steadily occupied more and more territory heavily populated with political opponents, who were brutally dealt with. The "White Terror" was under military control almost from the beginning and became an institutionalized process. During the first months, thousands of militiamen captured on the southern front were shot down en masse, while other thousands of political prisoners were killed by police and volunteer units. After the first few months, all political executions in the Nationalist zone had to be authorized by court-martial, but this reduced the rate of killings only slightly. There is no way of telling how many political prisoners were executed by the Nationalists before the war ended. A minimum estimate would be 40,000–50,000, and the true figure may be two or three times that.

By the autumn of 1937, Franco's forces had occupied the entire northern coastal zone, originally held by the Republic, and were almost ready to strike at the heart of the Popular Front's strength. The planned Nationalist winter offensive of 1938 was, however, forestalled by a Republican assault through the mountains southeast of Zaragoza. Franco scrapped his own plans and reshuffled his units to seal off the Republican breakthrough. By February 1938, all the ground lost had been recaptured, and the best enemy units were exhausted. The subsequent Nationalist offensive eastward from Aragon reached the sea by mid-April and cut the Republican zone in half. The last major effort of the Republican Army was made in the summer of 1938, when its final resources were mustered for a counteroffensive southwestward from Catalonia across the Ebro River to take the advancing Nationalists from the rear. This attack enjoyed only limited success; but, once more, Franco dropped his own plans to meet the Republicans on ground of their choosing. During a three-month struggle of attrition along the Ebro, the remaining combatworthy Republican units were ground down. When the Nationalist advance was resumed at the close of 1938, all Catalonia fell to Franco. The remaining Republican resistance in the central zone around Madrid collapsed during March 1939, amid bitter conflict between the Communist and anti-Communist Republicans. Franco insisted upon unconditional surrender and was able to announce the end of the Civil War on April 1, 1939.

Its cost in human lives has been a matter of debate ever since. Precise casualty statistics are not available, but it is clear that the death rate was not so high as in many other contemporary conflicts, because of lower firepower and looser military organization. The best evidence indicates that the Nationalist forces lost approximately 70,000 men killed or fatally wounded out of approximately one million mobilized. Of these fatalities, however, more than 2,000 were Italian and 300 were German, while as many as 15,000 may have been Moorish mercenaries. Republican military deaths were more numerous—according to one source, totaling 49,000 in 1937 alone, and altogether, may have reached 100,000 or more. Approximately 90 percent of the Republican war dead were Spanish, the remainder being from the International Brigades. Moreover, there were tens of thousands of political executions.

Franco won a total victory. The outcome was due at least as much to the inefficiency and internal rivalry that wracked the Popular Front as to the strength and ability of Franco's forces. His main personal contribution was to achieve and maintain political unity within his camp, concentrating the energies of the Nationalists on winning a military decision. This unity was gained not merely through dictatorship, but by establishing a Nationalist political community sufficiently broad and syncretistic to include all anti-Popular Front elements. Rather than relying on any one force, Franco drew them all together in an eclectic hodge-podge, with himself as arbiter. He was able to do this because he was military Commander-in-chief and not fully identified with any specific political sector.

Once the war was over, the dictatorship faced serious new problems. At least 10 to 15 percent of the nation's wealth, never great, had been destroyed. Much of the population remained hostile to the victorious regime, while the Nationalists, behind their façade of unity under Franco, were revealing internal division. So long as the war lasted, they had buried their differences for fear of a worse fate, but the unifying pressure had ended. Moreover, mounting tension in Europe threatened the outbreak of a major international war whose effects Spain was ill-prepared to withstand.

To counter these obstacles, Franco enjoyed greater personal power than any Spanish ruler since Fernando VII. He was the only leader whom the victorious Nationalists had, for very nearly every alternative had been eliminated by the Civil War. Though a minority of the supporters of the Popular Front remained intensely hostile, most were sunk into a sullen apathy, in no condition to contest the will of the victors.

Yet, despite the broad extent of his personal powers, Franco was at something of a loss as to how to use them. The end of the war made it possible to begin in earnest the construction of a Falangist syndicate system, but this merely took the form of government-dominated labor unions organized to keep the workers in line. The reform projects of "left" Falangists mostly were ignored, for this would have antagonized the coalition of conservative elements upon which the regime was based. Government agencies did take the lead in granting credits to help rebuild devastated areas, but they could not provide much assistance unless the regime were to embark on a drastic reorganization and redistribution of wealth. Though Falangist demagogy was of some value as propaganda to the government, this rarely went beyond rhetoric. Franco, who had no training whatever in economics, evidently expected the economy slowly to right itself, assisted only by marginal government efforts. In 1939, he spoke of at least five years of work being necessary before the level of 1935 could be regained. After the Second World War broke out, the resultant pressures and shortages delayed recovery twice as long.

In politics, Franco found no alternative to continuing the same kind of eclectic authoritarianism that had been developed during the Civil War. The monarchists hoped that an end to the fighting would make way for the restoration of D. Alfonso, but Franco had no such plans. In fact, his only real plan was to continue the present regime by hook or crook. The cabinet was reshuffled in August 1939, but the same balance between the generals and members of the various Nationalist civilian cliques was maintained. The Italian Foreign Minister, Ciano, who wanted Franco to give more clear-cut form to his government, wrote that the Spanish dictator seemed confused and uncertain as to how to proceed. In a sense, that was correct, but it implied no lessening of Franco's determination to maintain the authority of the regime in the aftermath of the Civil War. Rather, not seeing his way clearly into the political future, the Dictator picked his steps carefully, making as few changes as possible, striving always to retain the support of the various forces that composed the "Glorious National Movement."

The approach of a major war between Germany and the West European democracies filled him with alarm, for he feared that the latter powers might turn on Spain, which had adhered to the Germano-Italian Anti-Comintern Pact of February 1939. During the last week of August, Franco urged Mussolini to use his influence to relax tension between Germany and Poland, but he was completely helpless to influence the course of events. One year earlier, at the time of the Munich crisis, Franco had infuriated the German leaders by trying to establish a position of neutrality in greater European conflicts. Though Hitler might consider this betrayal, it was the only way for the Spanish regime to avoid the danger of being crushed between the great powers, as was soon to be the fate of so many small- and medium-sized countries.

The outbreak of the war in Europe had no immediate political or military effect on Spain. The regime quickly declared its neutrality, and the Western democracies had no desire to complicate their situation by antagonizing the Spanish dictatorship. During the period of the "phony war" (to May 1940), contacts with Germany were minimal. Spanish observers, like many others, had respect for the French Army and by no means regarded German victory as certain. Nor was opinion among the regime's supporters united about the desirability of a complete German victory. There was a strain of Anglophilia among the upper classes and even among a minority of the military.

An important factor in encouraging neutrality was the regime's relationship with Salazar's Portuguese government, which had always been close. The neighbor dictatorship, not unlike Franco's in its structure, had supported the latter throughout the Civil War. In March 1939, the two Iberian regimes had signed a treaty of friendship and non-aggression; and the independent, somewhat pro-British orientation of Salazar encouraged Franco's own sense of caution.

The first phase of the war ended with the smashing German breakthrough on the Western Front and the capitulation of France. The Spanish ambassador acted as go-between for the French leaders, in part because the Spanish government was eager to work out some sort of compromise that would preserve a balance of power in western Europe. The complete destruction of France would have left Spain too exposed to German pressure. The eventual armistice terms extended the zone of German occupation in France all the way down to the western tip of the Pyrenees, but left a conservative French dictatorship in control of the southeastern half of the country, preserving at least a minimal buffer.

German domination of nearly all western continental Europe abruptly changed the Spanish diplomatic position. Madrid's attitude, hitherto most correct and neutral, became distinctly pro-German. The Spanish position shifted from that of "neutrality" to "non-belligerence." Facilities for German submarines were provided in Spanish ports, and in July 1940, preliminary conversations began between Spanish and German officers concerning the possibility of a joint assault against the British bastion of Gibraltar, long coveted by Spanish nationalists. Nor did ambitions cease there. From the very beginning, there had been a note of imperialism in Falangist propaganda, which talked of extending Spanish influence over Latin America, of expanding Spanish power through the West Mediterranean and Northwest Africa, inheriting most of the remains of the French African empire. After mid-1940, this talk was greatly increased in volume and given a prominent place in the regime's propaganda. It was intended to mark out Spain's place in the "New Order."

The principal spokesman for the pro-Axis line was Serrano Súñer. In the process, he acquired an international reputation as the chief "Spanish Nazi"; but, in fact, his subsequent protestations that he disliked and distrusted the Germans seem to be truthful. Though he was the principal architect of Franco's FET, Serrano was not a radically nihilist Nazi-type fascist, but a more conservative sort of Catholic authoritarian, who might be compared with Dollfuss and Salazar (whence he drew some of his original inspiration). He felt much closer to the Italian Fascists than to the German Nazis. As he explained in his memoirs, he believed after the fall of France that German domination of the continent was inevitable and that Spain must make the best possible deal with Hitler in order to survive. To facilitate relations with the Germans, Franco appointed Serrano Foreign Minister in October 1940.

After being checked in the Battle of Britain, Hitler showed

interest in obtaining Spanish collaboration to reduce the remaining British strongholds in the West Mediterranean. However, Franco, as cautious as ever, did not share the absolute confidence in German victory held by some of the more extreme government and Falangist figures. Britain remained unconquered, and there was always a chance that the United States might come to her aid, fundamentally altering the balance of power. Moreover, by the autumn of 1940, the Spanish economy was in desperate straits. The disruption of international commerce brought about by the war severely hampered reconstruction in Spain, which faced great obstacles in any event. Weather conditions deteriorated in the early 1940's, by which time economic deprivation was actually worse than it had been during the Civil War. Spain was in no position to become involved in military adventures either from an economic or military point of view. With the close of the Civil War, German and Italian arms shipments had ceased, and the materiél of the Spanish Army steadily deteriorated. Therefore, when Hitler and Franco had their one and only personal meeting at Hendaye on the Spanish border, the German ruler was held at arms length throughout a day of detailed requests and tedious explanations. Franco agreed in principle to assist the German effort against Britain, but made this contingent upon massive shipment of foodstuffs and arms from Germany, as well as German agreement to a Spanish takeover of French Morocco and much of Algeria as well. Franco's reluctance, combined with excuses and stipulations, frustrated and infuriated Hitler. He promised vaguely to supply Spain with whatever was necessary, and a secret draft agreement was signed by the respective foreign ministries providing for Spanish participation in the war, but implementation was left contingent on the working out of details.

As the weeks passed, Franco's reluctance increased. It was clear that England would not fall during 1940, and Italy's invasion of Greece in the autumn of 1940 turned into a near disaster for Italian arms. All the while, German interest in Spain's participation remained fairly strong, even though Hitler was reluctant to meet Franco's price. German diplomats and generals wheedled, and the ambassador in Madrid, von Stohrer, complained that Franco was "isolated," talked to few people, and sometimes intervened in government affairs in a way that contradicted his supposed policies. However, Franco's personal "isolation" helped him avoid being unduly influenced by the omnipresent factionalism of the pro-Nationalist cliques, while his "contradictions" more often than not were intended to preserve the pragmatic balance of interests behind the regime, without leaning too far toward either Army extremists, Falangists, monarchists, or clerical reactionaries. During the winter of 1940–41, when Hitler seemed eager, Franco kept his price high. By April, after impressive German victories in Yugoslavia and Greece, the Spanish dictator showed more interest in coming to terms. However, Hitler was then busy preparing the invasion of Russia and no longer so concerned about the West Mediterranean.

The end of Hitler's pact with Stalin removed a major obstacle to closer association between Germany and the hyper-Catholic, intensely anti-Communist Spanish regime, while the initial German victories in Russia increased confidence in German victory. Though still not willing to enter the conflict officially, the Spanish government announced organization of a volunteer group that would fight beside the Germans in the east. By October, the "Blue Division" of 20,000 Spanish volunteers had taken up a position in the German lines near the northern end of the Russian front. Franco declared on July 17, 1941:

. . . The American continent cannot dream of intervention in Europe without exposing itself to catastrophe. . . . To say that the fate of the war can be changed by the entry of a third power is criminal madness. . . . The Allies have lost it. . . . In these moments . . . German arms are leading the battle for which Europe and our people have longed for so many years and in which the blood of our youth is going to be mingled with that of our comrades of the Axis, as a living expression of our solidarity. . . . Our movement achieves an unexpected vindication in the world today.

This peak of enthusiasm for the German war was soon reduced by the defeat before Moscow in December 1941. It became clear that final victory still eluded Hitler. During 1942, full Spanish participation seemed more attractive to the German government than it had in mid-1941, but by that time Franco had again raised his price to the maximum, and Hitler could scarcely have met it even had he been so disposed.

The entrance of the United States into the war drastically shifted the balance of power and presaged large-scale military operations in the West Mediterranean. Franco and Salazar responded by announcing in February 1942 the formation of an "Iberian Bloc" by their two regimes, with the aim of coordinating foreign policies to preserve the independence and neutrality of the peninsula. The Iberian Bloc became the Spanish regime's most enduring diplomatic association, and sixteen years later was expanded into a mutual defense treaty.

A domestic political shake-up took place in the late summer of 1942. Since the start of the regime, there had been strong hostility between Falangist extremists and the more conservative military and monarchist elements. In addition to differences over internal policy, the ultra-Falangists were pro-Nazi, whereas most conservatives favored continued neutrality. In August 1942, Falangists got into a brawl with Carlist youths in Bilbao where the ultra-conservative Minister of War, General Varela, happened to be visiting. Shots were fired, and a hand grenade was thrown. After this incident, Varela tried to mobilize Army opinion for disposing of Falangist "provocations" once and for all. In so doing, he overreached himself, seizing the political initiative without Franco's prior approval. On the other hand, Franco could not ignore the complaints of the generals and conservatives, who hated Serrano and the fascistic elements. He responded by striking a new balance. The two leading Army officers in the cabinet, Varela and Galarza (Interior Minister), were both dismissed to show that the Falangists would still retain a degree of influence. More important, however, was the removal of Serrano Súñer as Foreign Minister, together with the dismissal of several of Serrano's leading Falangist appointees. The usefulness of the Dictator's brother-in-law had ended. While playing a vital role in creating the regime's initial structure, he had been held responsible for many decisions and had become the most hated figure in Spanish government. His pro-Axis policy was useful in 1940–41, but after the German stalemate in Russia and the United States' entry into the war, this, like Serrano's domestic manipulations, was more of a liability than an asset. His dismissal was interpreted abroad as a swing away from the Axis by Franco. To some extent, that was correct, but it was also a move to strengthen the domestic balance of the regime.

The Anglo-American offensive in North Africa in November 1942 did not prove alarming to the regime; for, at its inception, the United States' ambassador presented Franco with a personal letter from President Roosevelt stating that the operations were in no way directed against Spain and that the Allies had no intention of intervening in Spanish affairs. Though nearly all the wartime propaganda of the democratic and Communist worlds bracketed Franco with Hitler and Mussolini as a leading fascist dictator, Roosevelt's pledge was a virtual guarantee of the survival of the regime, at least so far as attacks from without were concerned.

As late as 1943, the German government made efforts to draw Spain into the war, talking of secret weapons that would turn the tide; but by that time, Franco had no intention of becoming involved. During the years 1942–44, Spain became the scene of an economic tug-of-war between German and Anglo-American importers, who vied for the purchase of Spanish pyrites and tungsten, vital to munitions making. The Spanish government export commissions sold to the highest bidder, driving prices to previously unimagined heights.

After Italy withdrew from the war at the beginning of September 1943, some of the privileged elements in Spain became very restive. Most of them did not know of Franco's guarantee from Roosevelt, but feared that unless steps were soon taken to "de-fascistize" the dictatorship, the whole regime would be overthrown by the triumphant anti-fascist international coalition. For most of the conservatives behind Franco, the alternative was restoration of the monarchy. If a change were to be made in the dictatorship, the only decisive influence would be that exerted by the military hierarchy, which had brought Franco to power in the first place. A few days after Italy's capitulation, most of the ranking lieutenant generals signed a carefully worded, respectful letter to Franco, reminding him of the way in which he had been elected Generalissimo and asking if he did not agree that the time had finally come to restore the monarchy. Franco received each of the signatories individually, informed them of his pledge from Roosevelt, adding that it was not fully clear that Germany had lost the war, anyway. He stressed the difficulties of the present situation, saying that a monarchy restored amidst the uncertainty and economic misery of those months would face almost insurmountable obstacles. None of the Army leaders had the courage to face up to Franco. So long as he preserved the privileges of the military hierarchy and their special role in the dictatorship, none of them was willing to gainsay him.

Monarchists made several efforts to bring pressure against Franco between 1943 and 1945, but all failed. The idea of a restoration had enjoyed only modest support in the country as a whole, while the key elements in the regime were either opposed to, or lukewarm regarding, the monarchist cause. Moreover, the latter was split between the traditionalist Carlist and the more moderate supporters of the main branch of the dynasty. All machinations were easily repressed, and Franco was still firmly in control when the European conflict ended in May 1945. The defeat of Nazi Germany marked the end of the formally "fascistic" period of the dictatorship. As early as 1942, a tendency to downgrade overt identification with fascism and the fascist powers was noticeable. During 1942–43, the regime took the first step toward a superficial constitutionalism by introducing a national assembly, or "Cortes." All candidates were either nominated or appointed by state organs, and the voting for those to be "elected" was strictly limited on a corporative basis, so that Franco's Cortes was tightly controlled from the outset. It was given the nominal right to approve new legislation, all of which originated in the executive branch of the dictatorship.

A further step in the superficial "liberalization" of the regime was taken in 1945, with the promulgation of a "Fuero de los Españoles," a sort of "Spanish Bill of Rights." This was intended to reassure Spaniards and the world about the constitutionality of the regime's civil procedures. Most civil liberties were conceded in principle, but massive obstacles remained in the provisions for summary prosecution of those guilty of "crimes against the fatherland," which could be interpreted as free speech and political dissidence. The "Fuero" was another dab of icing on the cake of dictatorship.

There was a great deal of tension in Madrid during 1945, for no one could be sure that the victorious anti-fascist allies would not move to overthrow the Spanish regime after having finished with Nazi Germany. The Soviet Union was particularly active in generating pressure against Spain, and Communist and Anarchist guerrillas moved back across the Pyrenees by the hundreds to foment rebellion. Franco was apprehensive, not merely of international pressure from without and leftist revolt from within, but also of efforts from monarchists to convince Army and civilian leaders that a Bourbon restoration was the only way to

avoid foreign intervention. The cabinet was reorganized, dropping the overt monarchists and further reducing Falangist influence. Several "neutral" technical specialists were brought in, and
an appeal was made to Catholic opinion by the appointment of
a "Catholic Action" leader, Alberto Martín Artajo, as Foreign Minister.

Franco's specious political changes had no effect on foreign
opinion. In 1946, the United Nations voted formal censure of the
regime and advised its members to withdraw diplomatic recognition from Spain. By the end of the year, France formally closed
the Pyrenean border. Spain was left in almost complete diplomatic isolation, the political pariah of western Europe.

During this critical period, Franco relied on steady nerve and
the assurance earlier given him by Roosevelt. He was immensely
aided by the fact that no organized, effective political alternative existed in Spain. The leftist opposition was seriously
divided and under police control. The Republican Government-
in-exile was a mere committee without genuine support, while
the monarchists lacked unity, leadership, and commitment. None
of the disparate elements that had supported the Nationalist
movement had been completely alienated by Franco; and, without any organized alternative, none of them was willing to take
a leap into the political unknown by repudiating the regime.
Most important, the Army remained loyal. Some lieutenant generals retained contact with the monarchists, but it was clear that
unless an absolute crisis occurred, they would make no move of
their own against Franco. Moreover, international ostracism enabled the regime to portray the foreign anti-fascist exclusion of
the Spanish dictatorship as an insult to Spanish dignity and
honor, to present the "Caudillo" as a national hero victimized
by the Black Legend and the "eternal enemies of Spain." This
line was, to some extent, effective in rallying neutral domestic
elements to the regime or, failing that, in encouraging them to
remain within their apolitical neutrality.

The only foreign governments to support the Spanish regime during these years of isolation were the fellow Hispanic dictatorships of Salazar in Portugal and of Juan Perón in Argentina. The Peronist regime offered more than diplomatic support, for Argentina had stored up sizable surpluses of meat and grain by the end of the World War and made large shipments on very easy terms during the middle and late 1940's. Moreover, Perón professed to find a strong affinity between his own system of authoritarian nationalism and demagogy and Spanish national syndicalism. Argentine assistance was important both in feeding the hungry Spanish people and in shoring up the morale of the regime's supporters. It was climaxed by a sumptuous state visit of Eva Perón to Madrid in 1947, at the height of the period of diplomatic ostracism.

To reassure conservatives, Franco took another step to institutionalize his regime in 1947. A national plebiscite of questionable validity ratified a "Law of Succession," which defined Spain as a "kingdom," with the dictatorship fulfilling the functions of a regency. Franco reserved for himself the right to name his successor, but the Law of Succession authorized creation of a twelve-man Council of the Realm—each member of which would be appointed directly or indirectly by Franco—to assist him in certain functions of the supreme executive power (*Jefatura del Estado*). According to the Law of Succession, should Franco become incapacitated, the vacancy of the executive power might be recognized by vote of the other ministers, the Council of the Realm, and the Cortes. A special three-man Regency Council, consisting of the President of the Cortes and the senior prelate and senior general in the Cortes, would then take charge of the government in order to transfer power to the successor previously designated by Franco. Should the latter not have chosen anyone, it would be the responsibility of the Council of the Realm to select by at least a two-thirds vote, subject to the approbation of the Cortes, a successor who must be a Spanish male "of royal lineage," Catholic, and at least thirty years of age, and willing to swear allegiance to the fundamental laws and principles of the regime. If an acceptable royal candidate could not be found, another regent might be named, again subject to approval by the Cortes within eight days. The "Law of Succession," with its complex provisions, was not designed to increase the influence of the monarchists so much as to solidify the dictatorship, allaying worries of moderates about the ultimate course of political responsibility.

The regime was redeemed from pariah status by the intensification of the Cold War. Franco had been calculating on some such development at least since 1943, when he urged a separate peace between Germany and the Western powers so that Hitler could concentrate against the Soviet Union. By the late 1940's, right-wing spokesmen in the United States liked to describe Franco as the "only general who had ever completely defeated the Communists"; and, after the Truman Doctrine and the beginning of the Berlin blockade, it became increasingly difficult for the American government to ignore the Spanish regime. With the development of NATO, there was pressure from military leaders to include Spain and considerable stress on the strategic importance of the Iberian peninsula. The French border was reopened in 1948, and diplomats from most of the major powers were back in Madrid by 1949. By that time, the Spanish government had negotiated a sizable loan from New York banks, and the American military had established initial contacts with their Spanish counterparts.

As the political pressure ended, the economic situation also began to improve. The strikes and public demonstrations that occurred in Barcelona and several other northeastern cities in 1951 were more a response to relaxed police activity and to inflation than a dramatic revival of the leftist opposition. This flurry no doubt encouraged Franco to undertake the cabinet reorganization that followed, but the new government reflected no significant policy changes. Two monarchist ministers were brought into the cabinet, several ultra-conservatives were dropped, and further gestures were made toward Catholic moderates. Having weathered the dark years of the 1940's, Franco saw no need to alter his existing political combination.

Formal negotiations for military aid and the establishment of military bases by the United States were begun in 1951, resulting in the signing two years later of a ten-year treaty of economic assistance and military cooperation. Although this did not constitute an official military alliance on the level of NATO, it provided for the construction of three major Strategic Air Command bases in Spain under joint Hispano-American sovereignty, a large American naval base on the south Spanish coast, and sizable economic aid for both the armed forces and the domestic economy. Though democratic and leftist influences in western Europe made it impossible for Spain to be admitted to NATO, the American pact greatly strengthened the political and diplomatic position of the regime. Moreover, by 1965, it had provided approximately $1.8 billion in military and economic assistance.

When the original treaty was renegotiated in 1963 for another five years, the quantity of economic aid was reduced, but the status of Spain's relationship with the United States was nominally enhanced by creation of a Joint Consultative Committee to discuss mutual problems between the two countries. Though this still did not technically constitute a full-fledged alliance, the renewal of the treaty specifically stated that any threat to Spain itself would be viewed as a matter of "common concern" by the United States Government. As relations between the United States and France deteriorated in the mid-1960's, Spain assumed increasing importance as a potential peg on which to base one corner of a revamped system of collective security in western Europe.

During the second decade of its existence, the regime had adopted the posture of a pragmatic, middle-of-the-road authori-

6.45

tarian state, not fascist, but resolutely anti-Communist, with the stress on domestic development and survival. Its only significant diplomatic initiative lay in relations with the Arab world. Earlier, during the Civil War, Nationalist propaganda stressed the community of interests and understanding supposedly existing between Spain and Muslim North Africa. By clever bargaining with Moorish leaders, Franco had maintained the loyalty of the Spanish Protectorate in north Morocco and won 70,000 mercenaries for the Nationalist Army. Hitler's reluctance made it impossible to increase Spain's African empire during the Second World War, except for the temporary occupation of the international zone of Tangier. After 1945, however, the regime still held the Protectorate, the enclave of Ifni farther down Morocco's Atlantic coast, the large barren region of Río de Oro (also known as the "Spanish Sahara") to the south, as well as Spanish Guinea and the island of Fernando Po along the coast of Tropical West Africa.

Despite Spain's position as a European "imperialist" power in Northwest Africa, Franco endeavored to pose as protector of Arab interests. This was all the easier in the late 1940's, since the Spanish regime and the states of the Arab Near East shared a common animus against the dominant countries of western Europe. Even in the 1950's, however, Spanish authorities permitted Moroccan nationalists to use the Spanish Protectorate as a staging base for their struggle against French control of the rest of the Sultanate, provided that none of their actions were directed against the government of the Spanish Zone. The regime calculated that France's position in Morocco was so strong that it could not be easily undermined, so that Spain in the meantime might improve its standing with Moroccan nationalists without endangering its own holdings. The French decision to withdraw from Morocco in 1956 apparently caught the Spanish government by surprise. Since there was little prospect of retaining the Spanish Zone in the face of an otherwise united and independent Morocco, the Protectorate was hastily relinquished in the spring of 1956.

For the leaders of the Spanish Army, this may have been the most unpopular single step taken by the regime since the end of the Civil War. However, the government soon showed that it had no intention of surrendering its other African possessions—at least for the moment—and repulsed an invasion of Ifni by Moroccan volunteers in the winter of 1957–58.

During the following decade, the government made a skillful and concerted effort to improve its image as an "enlightened" colonial power. Significant sums were invested in the small remaining colonies to accelerate their economic development, so that per capita income in Spanish Guinea and Fernando Po became the highest of any region in West Central Africa. Local African leaders were given prominent positions in administration, and plans were announced for the further evolution and eventual emancipation of the colonies. After the repression of rebel movements in the Portuguese colonies brought almost universal condemnation of the Portuguese regime in the 1960's, the Spanish government carefully avoided identifying itself with the Portuguese position. Though Franco occasionally pronounced words of sympathy and consolation for his fellow dictator in Lisbon, it became clear that the Spanish government had no intention of backing up Portugal's colonialist stand with either men or money.

Following the advent of the Gaullist Fifth Republic in France in 1958, Spain's association with its northern neighbor became closer. One of the aims of De Gaulle's "independent" foreign policy was to draw Spain away from the United States and into the orbit of a French-led western Europe. At the same time, the West German government increased military and economic association with Spain and showed itself willing to back Spanish entry into NATO and the European Common Market. Over a period of fifteen years, international ostracism had changed into a multiplicity of competing friendships, leaving the Spanish regime more secure and independent than ever before.

The varied interests that had supported the dictatorship during the Civil War and after could have little quarrel with Franco's conduct of foreign affairs, and their disunity in domestic politics was such that scarcely any of them dared take an independent position. After twenty years, some of the original pressure groups had begun to dissolve. The government's own party, the Falange, was in a state of decay, leaving a number of the movement's original leaders embittered and disillusioned. The remaining cadre of Falangist militants was capable, however, of provoking one last crisis in 1956, after a small riot at the University of Madrid between pro- and anti-Falangist students. A group of Falangist extremists apparently made plans to express their political frustration by liquidating certain leaders of the liberal opposition. At this point the Army hierarchy intervened, and Franco ordered the Falangists restrained.

Yet the progressive de-falangization of the dictatorship raised the question as to whether the regime any longer possessed a coherent structure or ideology. The eclectic composition of Franco's cabinets and the opportunistic compromises of his policies left even his supporters hard put to make a viable definition of the regime and its structure. If the dictatorship's enemies could not overthrow it, the regime might eventually founder through a combination of apathy, corruption, and its own amorphousness. The Falange was, for better or worse, the only organized politico-ideological force totally committed to the regime. Consequently, Franco recalled to office José Luis de Arrese, who had earlier served nine years as a trusted and loyal Secretary General of the Party, and gave him the task of working out some kind of viable new political arrangement for the Falange and the state in the liberalized atmosphere of the 1950's.

A special conference of Falangist leaders was summoned, and as it turned out went farther than Franco had probably intended. The Falangists drew up a project that provided for the "constitutionalization" of the regime, but under the permanent control of a Falangist oligarchy. It was proposed to democratize elections to the Cortes, but only for members of the FET; to create the separate post of Prime Minister with a cabinet responsible to the legislature, but again responsible to a all-Falangist legislature. These proposals were inherently unrealistic, if for no other reason than that membership in the FET had dropped drastically since the 1940's and included only a small minority even of that sector of the population that supported the regime. Such a falangistization of the dictatorship was vigorously opposed by the regime's other pressure groups, led by the Army and the Church, and Franco finally ordered the proposals to be dropped.

When the cabinet was reorganized in 1957, Franco increased the role of Army leaders and, in accord with his policy of relying upon ultra-Catholic elements, brought a new group into the limelight—the semi-secret Catholic lay order, Opus Dei. This organization was founded by an Aragonese priest in 1929, but achieved prominence only after the Civil War. Its goal is to increase the influence of Roman Catholicism in political, economic, and cultural affairs, proselytizing among the elite elements of society. The great majority of its members, whether or not they have taken vows of celibacy, carry on secular careers in economic or cultural pursuits. By the 1950's, the Opus group numbered business leaders and intellectuals of note in its ranks and did everything possible to promote them into positions of influence. The political ideals of the order's most prominent members are clerical, elitist, authoritarian, and technocratic. Though the leading Opus intellectuals are monarchists, those members in positions of political and administrative power have seemed more interested in making an authoritarian, pro-Catholic system function in harmony with contemporary economic demands than in restoring the throne. The Opus group appeared eminently useful to Franco as a partial replacement for old-line Falangists, and Opus experts were given the posts for economic affairs in the 1957 cabinet. Franco thus maintained the syncretistic structure of his regime, adjusting it to face the more technical problems of the late 1950's without conceding any of his ultimate sovereignty. This tendency was successfully emphasized two years later, when it became necessary to liberalize the ecenomic controls that had been maintained for two decades. The subsequent cabinets of 1962 and 1965 were filled increasingly with technical experts from the safe sectors of politics and society, underlining the supposedly "apolitical" character of the dictatorship and its theoretical preoccupation with problems of national development.

Not the least of the paradoxes of a regime that began as a military dictatorship has been the scant difficulty the dictatorship has had with the military. Bad relations between politicians and soldiers are more commonly the fault of politicians than of soldiers. The conspicuous role the Spanish Army has played in the country's public affairs during the nineteenth and twentieth centuries has been due as much or more to the weakness of the political structure as to the ambition of Army leaders. Under the Franco regime, the senior generals have enjoyed a special relationship with Franco that has given them greater potential veto power than any other single group, not excluding the Church hierarchy; but the Army, as such, has never been confused with the political structure of the state. The very opposite has been encouraged, until by the 1960's it might be said that the Spanish Army Officer Corps had become more strictly professional and apolitical than at any time in its modern history. Spanish leftists have bitterly denounced the concept of civic responsibility that led a large part of the military to rebel against the liberal Republic in 1936. Thirty years later, they denounced the absence of any distinct sense of political role among officers, since this meant that the Army could scarcely be used to bring an end to the regime through an old-fashioned *pronunciamiento*. Not merely did Franco have little political difficulty with the armed forces; but, by the 1960's, they were even costing his government proportionately less than the outlays in the Republic's military budget, for much of the expense of modernizing the Spanish military in the 1950's and 1960's was borne by the United States.

For the first time in the history of the regime, Franco took the step in 1962 of appointing a Vice-Premier who might serve under the Law of Succession as his temporary successor in case of incapacity. The choice fell on Lt. Gen. Agustín Muñoz Grandes, an old comrade from Morocco and the Army's most influential senior commander. Muñoz Grandes' role in case of emergency would be to assume Franco's powers temporarily or, in the event of Franco's death or permanent incapacity, to set in motion the mechanism created by the Law of Succession to install a permanent successor. Muñoz Grandes was only one year younger than Franco, and his health was distinctly more precarious. His nomination posed no threat to Franco's sovereignty, but served to reassure the Army and other conservative groups about the stable continuity of the regime's authority.

Though in the early years of his regime Franco made frequent verbal references to the ideal of a totalitarian, fully mobilized society, in practice he had always made it clear that the Nationalist dictatorship was a pragmatic proposition, not a doctrinaire, ideologically circumscribed government. The eclectic character of the regime is well illustrated by the tabulation of the political background or identification of Spanish cabinet members from 1938 to 1962, seen in Table 1.

By the 1960's, the term "evolution" had become common among the regime's apologists. Bureaucratic and judicial controls had been relaxed considerably during the previous decade, and the area of personal autonomy enjoyed by private citizens in their individual affairs had significantly increased. The de-em-

TABLE 1

	Total	% of
Falange:		
Falange with no previous political background	8	12
Falange with CEDA background	5	7
Technical with Falangist orientation	4	6
Total Falange	17	25
Carlist	3	4.5
Acción Española and non-Carlist Monarchist	2	3
Civil figures of the Primo de Rivera dictatorship	3	4.5
Political Catholicism	3	4.5
Opus Dei	3	4.5
Technical or civil service apolitical	10	15
Military:		
With Falangist leanings	3	4.5
With Carlist leanings	1	1.5
With Acción Española or Opus Dei ties	2	3
With CEDA background	2	3
Former office holders under Primo de Rivera	2	3
With no particular identification	16	24
Total Military	26	39
TOTAL	67	100 %

SOURCE: Juan J. Linz, "An Authoritarian Regime: Spain," in E. Allardt and Y. Littunen, *Cleavages, Ideologies and Party Systems. Contributions to Comparative Political Sociology* (Helsinki, 1964), 291-341.

phasis of ideology by the regime had been accompanied by the de-politicization of important sectors of Spanish life, while the number of issues that could be publicly discussed without censorship had noticeably increased. Only the most active and directly subversive political opponents were arrested; almost none were shot. Within the government press, there was more and more talk about "representative" policy. These factors and others were invoked to indicate how far the regime had evolved, how little remained of the old fascistoid dictatorship of 1939.

The one basic element that always remained unchanged was the Generalissimo's personal power. It had never been total, for it was limited by the concerns of the military hierarchy, by the interests and doctrines of the Church, and to some extent by economic groups. Yet Franco retained complete political authority. After new labor disputes in the 1960's and pressures from moderate elements, there was some talk in government newspapers of the need for "dialogue," even for "democracy" in decision-making, but not the slightest bit of official authority was being relinquished to make this possible. Rhetorical maneuvers of offering verbally with one hand what was withheld in practice by the other had been going on for thirty years and indicated no substantial change in the power structure of the regime.

A list of the factors that have made Franco's personal rule so viable over a period of thirty years would have to include the following:

1. The great gulf of fear and hatred created between the two opposing Spanish camps by the Civil War, which has discouraged pro-Nationalist elements from seeking other compromises or alternatives;

2. Franco's lack of any binding a priori ideological commitment, which has freed him from fixation upon any predetermined policy;

3. His clever tactical opportunism and skill in balancing and playing off the interests of the various pro-Nationalist elements;

4. His willingness to delegate authority over significant areas of administration to his own hand-picked subordinates, allowing them to make their own contributions or take the blame for unpopular policies, as the case might be;

5. Changes in the international situation entirely beyond

Franco's power to influence, but which have been made use of skillfully;

6. Exploitation of the social possibilities of a corporatist program;

7. The economic boom of the 1950's and 1960's;

8. The internal weakness of the overt opposition groups due to their disunity, the doctrinaire ideological goals of many of them, the fixation on the issues and problems of the Republic and Civil War to the exclusion of more recent developments, and the lack of awareness shown by most exile groups of the changes that have occurred within Spain;

9. The geographical location of Spain, which both gives it strategic value in world affairs and yet makes it easier to avoid involvement in great continental wars.

In 1962, the Generalissimo reached his seventieth birthday, his health no longer so secure as in former times, but still relatively vigorous. Though there were indications that he was under no illusion as to the shortcomings of certain aspects of his regime, to relinquish power had become unthinkable. It was claimed by many that Franco had become convinced by the regime's own propaganda about the Divine Grace that had made him Dictator—that he felt himself to have been chosen by the hand of God. It is impossible to gauge fully this aspect of his personal conviction, but it was fully clear that there was no slackening of his will or confidence in his personal command.

c

3 / The Spanish Economy Since the Civil War

The political propaganda of the 1930's had the effect of making every sector of Spanish politics more keenly aware of social problems—and of some of the economic factors underlying them —than ever before. In certain respects, the five years of the Second Republic (1931–36) constituted a period of economic depression. Though good weather kept agrarian production high, industrial output dropped nearly one-third from its peak in the 1920's. The slow pace of economic development and the maldistribution of national income were important factors in generating the antagonism that provoked the Civil War. In general, the capital-possessing elements supported the Nationalist movement, while the urban workers and the landless southern peasants backed the Popular Front.

In the face of the demagogy propounded by the leftist groups, the emergent military dictatorship could hardly propose mere reversion to the pre-Republican status quo. From the very beginning, the rebel generals spoke of the need for greater social justice and said that "honest gains" made by the working classes would be protected. The national syndicalist program of the Falange provided a version of the fascist corporate state made to order for a military dictatorship seeking means to direct and control the economy and particularly to restrict the demands of the working classes.

Falangist national syndicalism meant, in theory, the construction of a broad series of vertical syndicates representing both workers and employers to coordinate the entire economy under the patronage of the state. It also advocated agrarian reform and irrigation projects and proposed to speed up industrialization. Thus, the Falangist program offered the ideal of what might be called a "development dictatorship," designed to lift the country out of its social and economic doldrums, which provided excellent talking points for government propagandists during the Civil War. The reality was quite otherwise, however, for the principal use of national syndicalism during the Civil War was development of state-controlled syndicates to dominate and regulate the workers in place of the Popular Front organizations.

Economic activity was carried on very much as usual in the Nationalist zone while the Civil War lasted, for that sector was composed mainly of grain-producing and other agricultural areas. Harvests were fairly bountiful and there was no food shortage on the Nationalist side. As the industrial areas originally controlled by the Republicans were occupied, more complex social and economic problems had to be faced. The availability of raw materials, markets, skilled labor, and qualified management had all been reduced by the war. Critical shortages in these areas, together with the destruction of property, resulted in a gross national product that was considerably smaller than in 1935.

The basis of the economy at the close of the Civil War was still agriculture, and the problem of agrarian reform had been debated by progressivist groups for several decades. The struc-

ture of landholding and cultivation in Spain is varied and may be divided into at least five different zones: 1) areas of tiny, subeconomic peasant holdings or minifundia, too small for mechanization or rational cultivation, located especially in the northwest but found also in other parts of northern and central Spain; 2) a larger sector of predominantly small family farms, devoted mainly to cereals (or to other grains, vineyards, or cattle), with little or no irrigation but with some potential for development, occupying much of northern Spain; 3) several small regions of small- to medium-sized holdings in irrigated areas, especially the *huerta* of Valencia and part of the valley of the Ebro, which have the highest rate of agrarian productivity in the country; 4) the sector of medium-sized farms, usually without irrigation, located in central and northern Spain, with enough acreage in many cases to encourage mechanization; and 5) the area of latifundia in southern, southwestern, and central Spain.

Before the Civil War, less than half the rural population owned any land at all, but the landowning peasantry, which numbered approximately one-third of the rural inhabitants, was nonetheless a capital-possessing class and, despite its low income, was relatively conservative politically. The larger landowners were overwhelmingly opposed to the Republic and its halting efforts at land reform. In the interest of owners of medium- and large-sized properties, all Republican measures of land reform were abolished by the rebel regime in the first weeks of the Civil War. In contrast to sometimes energetic efforts to encourage more rapid industrialization, very little was done by the regime to re-structure landowning and agrarian production until the 1950's. Since that time, a great deal of reforestation has been completed; and, during the eleven years 1954–65, more than one million hectares* of small scattered peasant holdings, mostly in northern Spain, were consolidated. Some progress has been made with

* One hectare is slightly less than 2.5 acres.

new irrigation projects, and the government has also purchased several large estates to resell to landless peasants, but the effects of these last two endeavors have been little more than marginal.

Consequently, the division of land ownership and exploitation in 1964 remained much the same as it had been thirty years earlier (see Table 2). Thus some 65 percent of the owners and

TABLE 2

Size of unit	Number of owners or renters	Total amount of land
Under 5 hectares	1,831,000	2,980,000 hectares
5–20 hectares	709,000	7,138,000 hectares
20–100 hectares	245,000	9,447,000 hectares
100 hectares and more	52,000	24,340,000 hectares

SOURCE: *Anuario Estadístico 1964.*

renters hold less than 7 percent of the arable land in tiny plots averaging little more than one and one-half hectares each, too small for the most efficient methods of cultivation. On the other hand, 1.8 percent of landowners still possess well over half the cultivated land. Moreover, in many cases, the land held by the large owners is relatively more fertile than that possessed by small farmers.

At the close of the Civil War, the rural economy produced the greater share of the gross national product and the majority of Spanish exports. Nonetheless, because of the social and political implications of the agrarian problem and the political influence of the larger landowers, little stress was placed upon capital investment in agriculture to change its structure or increase efficiency. Table 3 shows the figures published by the prominent economist Higinio París Eguilaz on relative investment in agriculture during the earlier years of the regime.

TABLE 3

Year	Total national investment (in millions of pesetas)	Investment in agriculture	Percentage of total investment devoted to agriculture
1942	5,215	386	7.4
1943	8,463	390	4.6
1944	7,719	482	6.2
1945	9,316	662	7.1
1946	10,592	793	7.4
1947	12,213	988	8.1
1948	15,609	1,013	6.5
1949	15,875	1,224	7.7
1950	18,217	1,566	8.5
1951	22,464	1,792	7.9
1952	25,775	3,005	11.6
1953	29,244	3,690	12.6
1954	34,343	4,513	13.1

Hence it was not surprising that Spanish agriculture remained much less productive than that of most of the rest of western Europe. During the period 1954–58, wheat productivity in various countries compared as shown in Table 4.

TABLE 4

	Yield per hectare in quintales (100 kilos)
Denmark	36.7
United Kingdom	27.8
France	19.5
United States	11.4
Spain	9.6
Portugal	7.8

For years, the general level of agrarian production remained lower than before the Civil War, as the figures in Table 5 indicate.

TABLE 5

Year	Indices of agrarian production	Population level (1931–35 = 100)	Agrarian production per capita
1940	82.8	106	78.1
1945	72.5	110	65.9
1950	86.5	115	75.1
1955	104.9	119	88.2
1958	117.3	122	96.1

SOURCE: Spanish Ministry of Agriculture.

This is not to contend that no improvement took place in agricultural techniques during the 1940's and 1950's, for mechanization increased in certain areas. According to the Ministry of Agriculture, the number of tractors employed rose as follows:

1940	4,300
1950	11,600
1955	26,000
1960	40,000

The slow spread of mechanization did not reach the ordinary peasant farmer, who, during the general Spanish price inflation of the 1950's, was caught in the urban-rural "price scissors" that has afflicted agrarian populations throughout the world during the past century. Table 6 shows the disproportionate increase in

TABLE 6

	(1940 = 100)		
Year	Food price level	Industrial price level	General level
1945	174.5	171.8	173.2
1950	321.6	339.8	329.7
1955	407.7	563.2	477.7
1957	502	738.1	608.4
1959	604.8	776.8	682.3

SOURCE: Instituto Nacional de Estadística.

prices. Mounting pressures against small farmers and landless peasants, combined with the lure of an increasing number of urban industrial jobs, both in Spain and abroad, have resulted in a general flight from the land. This began decades earlier, but reached mass proportions during the 1950's and 1960's. Altogether, as Table 7 indicates, during the quarter-century 1940 to 1965, about one-third of the active rural population either moved to the cities or emigrated.

TABLE 7

Year	Percentage of Spain's active males in agriculture and fishing	Percentage of annual change	Number of active males in agriculture in thousands	Index (1900=100)
1900	61.4	−	3,782	100
1910	58.9	− 0.25	3,861	103
1920	61.6	− 0.27	4,233	112
1930	50.7	− 1.09	4,450	118
1940	54.8	.41	4,519	120
1950	53.2	− 0.6	4,853	128
1960	42.0	− 1.12	4,024	107
1964	36.5 °	− 1.62	3,254	86
1970	27.0 °°	− 1.58	2,500	66

SOURCES: Instituto Nacional de Estadística, *Anuario Estadístico 1963; Avance del Censo de Población de 1960.*
° Last quarter of 1964, Instituto Nacional de Estadística, *Encuesta sobre la Población Activa en 1964.*
°° Estimates by Amando de Miguel (DATA, S. A., Madrid), who also compiled the preceding material.

Throughout the years of the Franco regime, a struggle has gone on within the government between those who want to use the powers of dictatorship for an actively interventionist plan of economic development and those elements that resist concerted change of the status quo. The relative neglect of the rural economy has been due not merely to the influence of wealthy landowners in blocking reform but also to the fact that Franco's government, like most twentieth century authoritarian states, has been much more attracted by the glamorous goal of accelerating industrial growth than by the prosaic task of reorganizing peasant agriculture.

In the aftermath of the Civil War, when the Spanish economy faced weaknesses and shortages of almost every kind, the state developed a broad framework of controls and rationing. Structural controls required prior authorization by government agencies for new investments of more than 50,000 pesetas, established a preferential category of industries of "national interest" that received special financial and commercial advantages, and required that whenever possible all government agencies and public enterprises procure all their supplies and equipment in Spain. In general, the system of state controls arranged in 1939–40 looked toward a position of relative autarchy for Spain in a wartime world where economic interchange was gravely reduced. This framework functioned for exactly twenty years and, during the first decade, in an economy of extreme scarcity. In theory, food was strictly rationed, industrial supplies and raw materials allocated by state boards, import licenses and foreign exchange apportioned, wage rates and work opportunities subjected to regulation.

The state's bureaucratic personnel, however, lacked the training, traditions, morale, or the rigor to make such a tight system of controls effective. Corruption abounded, and loopholes were found on every hand. By the early 1940's, a massive black market, mainly in foodstuffs, had developed. Favoritism and influence-buying were not restricted to consumer necessities, but were part of the ordinary functioning of big business as well. Materials, import licenses, even labor relations, were major items for bargaining with officials high and low. Almost every department or regulatory agency dealing with the economy had its own "reserve" section of stocks or credit. These were not normally subjected to rigorous central auditing, and so became a source for large-scale graft and black market operation.

The controls of the Franco regime were imposed upon the economy from above and did not serve to change the basic structure of ownership in most sectors. Major enterprises learned to adjust to the system, and most small concerns also managed to get by, though with greater difficulty. If production did not increase, or even slumped, the margin of proportionate profit usually remained about the same. The original Falangist program called for nationalization of credit, but the Franco regime interfered comparatively little with the established functioning of finance. Total dividends of the larger banks had averaged 12 to 14 percent on capital during the 1920's, then had fallen to about 8 percent under the Republic. During the bleak years of the 1940's, they rose to the following figures:

1942	8.5%	1945	10 %
1943	9.36%	1946	10.35%
1944	9.75%	1947	10.83%

and remained at approximately this rate through the 1950's.

Both before the Civil War and after, much criticism has been heard about the "monopolistic" structure of Spanish industry and finance. A study in 1953 revealed that 9 of the 338 enterprises engaged in coal mining accounted for 55 percent of the total coal production; that 10 of the 40 steel-producing enterprises provided 82 percent of the steel production; that 14 of 511 electric power enterprises were responsible for 71 percent of the electrical production; and that similar degrees of concentration existed in certain other industries. Similarly, the five largest banks controlled from 45 to 60 percent of the capital invested in industry in Spain. At the same time, it should be pointed out that the big banks and their related enterprises have developed the most efficient economic operations in Spain and are responsible for impressive new projects, especially in hydroelectric development.

The preceding figures illustrate one major aspect of Spanish industrial structure, but such citations do not tell the whole story. In criticizing Spanish industrial organization, it is just as easy to stress the other side of the problem and say that the proliferation of uneconomically small shops and factories is the true obstacle to the rationalization of Spanish industry, for the number of small enterprises that turn out the remainder of industrial production is extraordinarily high. According to the 1960 industrial statistics, there were 22,000 small metallurgical shops that employed, on the average, three workers each. In the chemical industry, 4,613 producers, the bulk of them in Catalonia, employed a total of only 14,574 workers. In the textile industry, where the absence of concentration has long been recognized as a problem, 4,500 of the total of 8,500 enterprises employed an average of less than ten employees each. Proportionately, it might be argued that there was more individual industrial entrepreneurship in Spain in 1960 than in the United States.

General industrial production did not regain the pre-Civil War level until approximately 1950. Low morale, absence or disappearance of skilled personnel, lack of raw materials and foreign assistance, scarcity of credit, disruption of markets, and low purchasing power all combined to retard recovery. During the mid-1940's, productivity in certain industries sagged disastrously, as the chart of productivity per hour in Table 8 indicates.

By the end of that doleful decade, many aspects of depression were being overcome. The resignation of the political opposition and increased imports and credit from abroad helped to improve the situation greatly, so that the 1950's were a period of expansion (see Table 9).

Increasing industrial production, together with opportunities

TABLE 8

	1929	1935	1940	1946	1947
Construction	100	102	52.5	52.5	52
Woolen goods	100	106.5	110	108	121
Iron	100	84.3	80.2	–	48.2
Shipbuilding	100	120	87.8	81	71
Heavy metallurgy	100	77.2	88.5	83.5	89.8
Light metallurgy	100	126	100	98	82
Electrical goods	–	100	73.3	83.8	77.5
Paper	100	97.5	98	116.5	105
Fertilizer	100	114	33.6	68.3	53
Chemical products	100	175	163	140	135

SOURCE: Published lecture by the economist Alejandro Suárez y Fernández Pello.

for work in other European countries, brought a general decline in unemployment. The number of registered unemployed decreased as follows:

1935	674,161
1939	441,388
1940	507,903
1945	163,759
1950	175,827
1955	111,207
1959	94,805

SOURCE: *Anuario Estadístico 1960.*

The government played a role in industrial expansion, not merely through its elaborate structural controls, but through direct investments in state capitalism. In 1941, the regime created a National Institute of Industry (INI) to develop entirely new stateowned enterprises in certain sectors or to buy shares in important concerns needing stimulation. During the 1940's, comparatively little money was available, but appropriations spurted

TABLE 9. INCREASE IN INDUSTRIAL PRODUCTION TO 1959

	Electrical energy	Coal	Non-ferrous metals
1929–31	100	100	100
1941–45	171	111	47
1946–50	230	156	51
1951	319	182	63
1952	362	198	67
1953	380	209	71
1954	395	212	75
1955	471	208	89
1956	534	220	96
1957	551	230	100
1958	610	238	111
1959	610	206	125
	Iron	Chemical products	Textiles
1929–31	100	100	100
1941–45	79	76	98
1946–50	84	95	98
1951	100	129	81
1952	113	183	99
1953	112	199	105
1954	135	214	96
1955	150	217	101
1956	152	214	106
1957	165	233	113
1958	195	258	128
1959	216	259	114

SOURCE: *Anuario Estadístico 1960.*

ahead in the following decade. Some INI activities were very wastefully and inefficiently conducted, but others resulted in important new industrial establishments. The most impressive was a new metallurgical complex in Asturias, ENSIDESA, which became the largest single steel and iron producer in

Spain. Despite complaints from private businessmen about the pressure of government competition, INI investments were increased to a total of approximately one billion dollars by the end of 1961.

In addition, the government also extended lesser amounts of credit to private enterprise through its "Banco de Crédito Industrial." The regime spent more money on the INI and other programs than it could afford, adding heavy costs of state investment to the high degree of corruption and waste present in most sectors of Franco's government. For twenty years, the dictatorship operated at an almost constant deficit.

This was due not merely to sloppiness, corruption, and poor planning, but to the narrowness of the tax base upon which the public treasury operated and the many gaps that were permitted. In a speech on December 22, 1948, an Undersecretary of Finance announced that the Spanish government took only 14.76 percent of the current national income in taxes, versus approximately 21 percent in France and Italy and 33 percent in Great Britain. Moreover, the bulk of this was collected in indirect taxes on goods and services, rather than direct levies on income and property. The social, as well as the financial, implications were obvious. The basic tax structure was not originated by the Franco regime but simply inherited from pre-Civil War governments, monarchist and republican. There is evidence, however, that the dictatorship has been considerably less rigorous than the Republic—and even more lax than the constitutional monarchy—in enforcing its own laws on direct taxation, particularly against the wealthier classes. Table 10 shows how the equivalent tax rates on the total value of national agrarian income and real estate have varied from year to year. A tax reform was effected in 1957, but its only purpose was to plug loopholes and relax pressure on certain kinds of industry that needed to develop a higher rate of investment. No effort was made to reverse the strongly regressive tendency of the tax

TABLE 10

	1929 = 100	
Year	Tax level on agrarian income	Tax level on real property
1930	101	102
1931	99	104
1935	113	111
1940	88	84
1941	87	82
1942	119	83
1943	112	76
1944	106	76
1945	104	73
1946	78	52
1947	81	58
1948	78	56
1949	87	47
1950	78	61
1951	59	52
1952	60	60
1953	60	66
1954	65	82
1955	67	94
1956	65	91
1957	57	77
1958	52	75
1959	54	77
1960	58	83
1961	57	87

SOURCE: *José Angel Sánchez Asiain*, "Análisis del sistema tributario español a través de la presión fiscal directa, aparente y real," *Anales de Economía*, II:1 (Jan.-Mar., 1963), 5-56.

structure, for it was calculated that indirect levies would continue to account for at least 55 to 60 percent of the total revenue.

With the government unable or unwilling either to collect

the funds to balance its budget on the one hand or to reduce expenses on the other, the printing of large amounts of new paper money became a standard feature of the regime's economics. This brought the price level higher and higher (see Table 11).

TABLE 11. PRICE INDEX, 1940–1959

1940 = 100

1940	100	1947	243.8	1954	459.8
1941	118.2	1948	261.1	1955	477.7
1942	130	1949	279.4	1956	521.3
1943	145.1	1950	329.7	1957	608.4
1944	156.1	1951	423.5	1958	668.2
1945	173.2	1952	427.1	1959	682.3
1946	207.8	1953	457.5		

SOURCE: *Anuario Estadístico 1960.*

Inflation did not at first retard industrial expansion. Indeed, it may to some extent have encouraged it. By 1957, however, galloping prices were getting completely out of hand. Furthermore, the foreign exchange rate was deteriorating as the international trade balance ran ever more heavily against the Spanish economy. Imports exceeded exports by the following percentages:

1931–35	125.59	1954	132.19
1941–45	97.04	1955	138.33
1946–50	118.09	1956	173.42
1951	83.24	1957	181.24
1952	126.73	1958	179.21
1953	126.42	1959	158.12

SOURCE: *Instituto Nacional de Estadística.*

By 1959, it was no exaggeration to say that the government itself was nearing bankruptcy, despite the impressive increase in the industrial economy. The gains made in certain sectors of domestic production could be marketed only within the country—thanks to the structural protection offered by the state system—but could not compete outside Spain. Yet sizable imports of raw materials and special equipment were necessary to maintain industrial growth. In this situation, it may reasonably be argued that only the rise of the tourist trade and the large-scale assistance of the United States permitted the unbalanced economy to move as far as it had.

There are indications that, for quite awhile, Franco—with his vague ideas about economics—did not understand how bad things were, but expected that the country could muddle through. Since the 1957 cabinet change, however, his government contained a new set of economics ministers with more precise, informed, and far-sighted views than their predecessors. They recognized that finances and commerce could not be allowed to deteriorate much further. A sizable foreign loan would be necessary to see the country through its current inflationary crisis and trade deficit. The United States Government and the International Monetary Fund indicated willingness to assist, but only if the Spanish Government undertook basic reforms of its own. After some debate, the Opus Dei economics ministers and like-minded colleagues managed to convince Franco that a fundamental revision of the regime's economic policies was needed.

The result was the Stabilization Plan of mid-1959. It marked an end to twenty years of pseudo-autarchy and removed or reduced many of the structural controls that had straitjacketed the economy. It would be an exaggeration to say that the new program reversed the direction of government policy, but it introduced basic alterations. By the close of the year, eighteen government control agencies had been abolished and a wide variety of items freed from regulation in domestic and foreign trade. Restrictions were placed upon credit, and the Bank of Spain's rediscount rate was raised from 5 to 6.25 percent. The peseta was devalued from the old nominal rate of 42 to a new ratio of 60 to the dollar, bringing it in line with market values and facilitating exports. Although one of the plan's fundamental goals was to improve the export-import balance, it was recognized that this could be done most effectively through an efficient, competitive free market economy. Spain became a full member of the Organization of European Economic Cooperation, and import licensing was therefore abolished on a total of 180 commodities deemed genuine import necessities, representing about 50 percent of the total volume of Spanish imports. Controls remained on less important items in order to protect foreign exchange, though it was planned that future improvements would make it possible to reduce or abolish these controls as well. To expand and modernize productive resources, investment of foreign capital was encouraged up to 50 percent of the total capital of any Spanish enterprise. In order to enable the national economy to withstand the current imbalance in the international level of payments and the transition to the new program, foreign loans totaling $548.3 million were negotiated by the government before the plan went into operation.

Internal Spanish investment was largely freed from government restriction, the minimum beyond which authorization was necessary being raised from 50,000 to 2 million pesetas. Special export credits and tax bonuses were arranged for firms that succeeded in exporting certain types of goods. More careful provisions were made for government industrial investment. At least temporarily, the rate would have to be reduced, and there was greater concern to coordinate it with the flow of private investment. The reduction of controls meant lowering of price restrictions on many commodities, with the result that prices on certain key items would continue to rise slightly, in line with their true market value, until a natural equilibrium was reached.

The Stabilization Plan "opened up" much of the Spanish economy for the first time in the history of the regime. The gains of the 1950's had been predicated, in some ways, on the artificial advantages of a closed system, hedged about by government protection and incentives. Significant progress had been made in certain areas, but inefficient practices in other sectors had been encouraged by the system. Therefore it was common for critics of the dictatorship to predict disaster for the government and the economy under the liberalization program.

This has not been the case. Contrary to many expectations, the Stabilization Plan proved a definite success. Initiation of the program did have a temporarily depressant effect in some industries, notably textiles. The unemployment rate rose slightly in 1959–60; and for the first time in more than a decade, per capita income declined—about 1.5 percent in 1960. However, the unemployment rate fell once more in 1961–62, and the rise in individual income was resumed. The inflation was brought to a complete halt in 1960. Though it reappeared in subsequent years, it was kept under control through the mid-1960's and never assumed the runaway proportions of the previous decade. The national budget was balanced in 1960 for the first time in years, and the foreign trade balance actually revealed a slight surplus. The Stabilization Plan proved effective in part because, by 1959, the quality of Spanish entrepreneurship had risen to a point where businessmen were able in many instances to take advantage of creative opportunities. Greater freedom under the new system, decreased margin for favoritism and corruption, a stronger trading position, availability of a reasonable amount of new capital, the extraordinary increase in the tourist trade—these factors all helped the economy to level out and advance to new heights in the 1960's (see Table 12).

During the same period, food production (shown in Table 13) also increased significantly.

The gross national product, based on the average of 1953–54, stood at 142.4 in 1959, then increased to 157.5 in 1961 and to 166.8 in 1962. Hence, though the cost of living increased

TABLE 12. INDUSTRIAL EXPANSION, 1959–63

| | 1958 = 100 | | | | |
	1959	1960	1961	1962	1963
General industry	102.8	105.2	123.2	134.5	144.8
Coal	91	90.3	92.4	88.6	90.8
Metals mined	97.7	106.2	110.2	102.4	95.1
Electricity	106.2	113.9	127.8	138.6	153
Gas	102.7	102.5	103.1	104.8	99.9
Food manufacturing	100.7	112.5	115.2	126.7	130.5
Textiles	94.1	96.2	105.9	112.9	113.4
Basic metals	125.8	115.3	160.3	160.1	168.6
Chemicals	111.7	117.9	132	143.1	159.3
Miscellaneous	102.3	100.4	120.7	139.5	156.1
Housing	98.9	92.9	107.4	127.3	—
Public works	105.2	108.7	128.1	162.3	—

SOURCE: *Anuario Estadístico 1964.*

TABLE 13. FOOD PRODUCTION, 1959–63

| | 1953–55 = 100 | | | | |
	1959	1960	1961	1962	1963
Farm products	123.5	115.4	124.2	129.5	149.2
Cattle	110.3	121.5	134.7	141.6	154.7
Total food production	119	117.5	127.9	133.7	151.1

SOURCE: *Anuario Estadístico 1964.*

more than 28 percent between 1958 and 1963, real income rose more rapidly (see Table 14).

These last statistics are, admittedly, somewhat misleading, for income in Spain is by contemporary Western standards maldistributed, and the income of the majority of the population not so high as per capita figures would indicate. During most of the period that Franco has been in power, opposition critics

TABLE 14. PER CAPITA INCOME, 1959–63

(in terms of the 1953 peseta)

1959	10,299 pesetas
1960	10,162 pesetas
1961	10,770 pesetas
1962	11,393 pesetas
1963	12,067 pesetas

SOURCE: *Anuario Estadístico 1964.*

customarily maintained that the living standards of the lower and lower middle classes have declined since the Civil War. By the 1960's, critics frequently had to concede that general living standards had risen, but centered their fire on the uneven distribution of increased production. The other side of the coin, of course, is the extraordinarily low productivity of Spanish labor compared with that of other Western countries. In 1959, it was estimated that, in the burgeoning Spanish steel industry, productivity per man-hour was only a little more than one-third of that in France or Belgium.

After 1959, the Franco regime placed much greater stress on economics than had earlier been the case. Spain, like most of the rest of the Western world, seemed to be entering a "post-ideological age," in which political utopianism had lost its meaning. The Generalissimo himself realized that politics per se were no longer the center of attention that they had been twenty years earlier, that the new post-Civil War generation of Spaniards was interested much more in higher living standards than in perpetuating the "spirit of the eighteenth of July." Political appeal was consequently becoming a matter of economic argument, with the regime's propagandists stressing steadily rising income and their opponents insisting that living standards were not improving quickly enough or for enough people.

To give more concerted direction to economic expansion,

Franco was persuaded in 1963 to adopt a four-year national economic plan, with a supervisory agency modeled on the Monnet planning commission (*commissariat du plan*) that had been organized to guide economic development in France under the Fourth Republic and after. One of the leading Opus Dei economists, Laureano López Rodó, was given cabinet rank as commissioner of the "Plan of Economic and Social Development," which projected a total investment of 5.5 billion dollars during the years 1964–67 inclusive.

Despite mounting unrest within the labor force, industrial expansion continued at an impressive rate in the more advanced sectors. New segments of the economy also moved forward; and, in shipbuilding, Spain ranked sixth in the world in gross tonnage at the end of 1965—ahead of the United States.

Economic planning was based on the assumption that increasingly closer association with the rest of western Europe was not merely desirable, but in the long run would be vital. In 1962, application was first made for associate membership in the Common Market. The goal was not full-fledged inclusion in the Common Market economy, for this would have exposed the economy to more competition than it could bear. Associate status, however, would have provided commercial advantages and established connections that would make full membership easier at a future date. Spain's application was, however, passed over for the time being because of French opposition to extension of the Market structure and because of the political criticism by the smaller democratic members. At the same time, regular commercial connections were developed with most of the Communist states of eastern Europe, including the Soviet Union. Though trade with the Soviet bloc accounted for only a minor share of Spanish foreign commerce, its development was of some significance as an example of the widening range of Spanish diplomatic and economic relations.

In foreign exchange, Spain's main reliance was on the extraordinary gold mine that had been developed in tourism. By 1965, the country was bidding to replace Italy and France as the single greatest travel attraction in western Europe. Some fourteen million visitors entered the country during that year, a total equivalent to more than one-third the population of Spain, and spent approximately $1.1 billion, far and away the largest single credit in the Spanish international balance of payments. Tourism was primarily, if not exclusively, responsible for the accumulation of gold reserves of more than $1 billion, which by 1963 had dramatically reversed the menace of bankruptcy that had hovered over the financial system six years earlier. The overwhelming success of the tourist industry was not, moreover, merely a matter of capitalizing on the exotic allure of "romantic Spain." By the 1960's, Spanish hotel management had become one of the best in the world, and great care had been taken to develop attractive, smoothly running, relatively low-cost tourist facilities of almost every kind. The record of Spanish enterprise compared with French stagnation in this regard was rather impressive, and not without reason could the Spanish National Tourist Commission send a technical aid mission to Argentina to provide expert advice on organizing the tourist industry.

A balance sheet of the Spanish economy in the 1960's would thus register definite points of strength, but grave weaknesses remain. Agriculture is as much the Achilles' heel of the economy in Spain as in the Soviet Union. Though general food production has increased more rapidly than the growth of population, the price scissors continues to trim profits and living standards for the bulk of the farm population. According to the Bank of Bilbao's statistics, the price differential has moved in the way shown in Table 15.

The only genuine profit realized from the agrarian economy is gained by a comparatively small minority of owners of large- and medium-sized farms, most of whom maintained their profit not simply by some effort at mechanization but also by

TABLE 15

Year	Prices paid by agrarian producers	Prices received for agrarian products	Parity index
1957	100	100	100
1960	142.8	117.6	82.4
1961	151.2	121.8	80.6
1962	166.1	132.5	79.8
1963	202.8	137.6	67.8
1964	223.1	143.4	64.3

paying agricultural laborers no more than the legal minimum, which was much lower than prevailing industrial wage rates. In 1965, agriculture still employed nearly 35 percent of the national labor force and accounted for a sizable share of Spanish exports, but received only about 25 percent of the national income, gross per capita income being less than two-thirds the national average. Weather conditions deteriorated in 1964 with a resultant sag in overall production. Despite provisions in the Four-Year Plan to increase agricultural investment and provide easier credit, opportunities for the small farmer and wage laborer remained meager. During 1965, there was a (probably temporary) decrease in the quantity of tractors and machinery purchased. In an earlier generation, the rural population would have had little alternative but to struggle and try to endure. But in the urban, industrializing Spain of the 1960's, there existed the possibility of higher wages or at least work in the cities; and the flight from the land accelerated, amounting to 200,000 people a year.

For years, Spanish economists have worried about "macrocephalic" over-concentration in half a dozen major areas: greater Madrid, greater Barcelona, the Bilbao-San Sebastián area, Valencia, and Seville. The per capita income of the industrialized provinces of Vizcaya and Guipuzcoa approaches the French national average, but that of the most backward agrarian districts may be compared with regions of the Middle East. Technocrats in charge of government planning are attempting to counterbalance these disparities by laying great stress on new growth centers located in or near agrarian regions that have heretofore been neglected. The greatest success has been the sudden burgeoning of the old Castilian capital of Valladolid as the center of a new light industrial complex. Significant results have also been achieved in developing the Burgos district. Other growth centers that receive special emphasis are La Coruña and Vigo in the northwest, the already partially developed city of Zaragoza in the northeast, and Huelva and Cádiz in the south.

Urban unemployment has been minimal in large part because of the massive emigration of un- and semi-skilled workers to the more advanced West European industrial areas. By 1966, it was estimated that 850,000 Spaniards, both male and female, were working in other European countries. In many cases, this resulted in a serious drain of semi-skilled labor, always in short supply in Spain. On the other hand, had it not been for this emigration, urban Spain could not have absorbed excess rural population so relatively well as it has. The consequence would have been massive aggravation of social ills. In addition, workers abroad have remitted savings to their families at home, further boosting the balance of payments. Yet it seems doubtful that Spain can continue to export labor in such quantities indefinitely. More jobs must be created at home, and the country will have to train and compete for much more skilled labor than in the past. Economic planning aims at doing just these things, but its long-range success remains problematical.

The tax structure remains regressive, with more than twice as much of the new increase in revenue coming from indirect levies as are raised by direct taxes. There seems little concern to deal with this problem, despite its social and economic consequences.

The favorable balance of international payments built up in the 1960's has rested on the spectacular profits of tourism more than on expanded exports. Though the latter have increased significantly, a more prosperous Spain has also accelerated its imports, so that by 1965 the trade balance had again grown slightly unfavorable, though it gave no immediate cause for alarm.

The attempted technocracy of government economic planning in the 1960's was a great improvement over the bumbling bureaucratic pseudo-autoarchy of earlier years, but it did not measure up to the level of precision and efficiency obtained by its French prototype. To some extent, this was neither surprising nor worthy of reproach, for statistical services and operative tools for planning simply have not been available to the extent found in the most advanced countries. Perhaps inevitably, wide disparities have appeared between calculations and goals on the one hand and actual achievements on the other.

Despite the gains made since 1950, it might be argued that the difference between the Spanish standard and that of most of the rest of western Europe was even greater in 1965 than in 1935. The level of entrepreneurial leadership, though rising, was still not on a par with that of the Common Market countries. The general ignorance and lack of technical training of the lower classes, together with the maldistribution of income, had still not been substantially overcome.

The regime, despite obvious efforts to speed development, cannot devote full attention to helping overcome the weaknesses in the Spanish economy, since it is ultimately based in large measure on the relatively immobile, oligarchic elements whose position the established order was to a considerable degree designed to protect. Though the dictatorship succeeds in repressing the economic disturbances of class struggle, to what extent its continuation constitutes any economic "advantage" is difficult to calculate. In its often fumbling, uncertain efforts to encourage greater production and well-being without changing the basis of property ownership or social distinction, the Franco regime is sometimes reminiscent of certain eighteenth-century governments that attempted a program of enlightened despotism while sustaining the basic structure of the old regime. Since those goals were ultimately contradictory, it did not really prove possible to realize the former—rationalization of administration and of usage of resources, together with a measure of social reform—until the latter—the old social and political order —had been either overthrown or substantially outgrown.

4 / Social Change

Despite all the rhetoric within and without Spain about the supposed "individualism" of Spaniards, Spanish society shows perhaps the greatest degree of adjustment to subgroup conformity found in any large Western country. Américo Castro has suggested that the key to Spanish history lies in the interaction of mutually exclusive castes during the Middle Ages, that Spaniards have defined their values and goals on the basis of their personality as part of their caste or group rather than on the basis of an empirical, individually objectified analysis of external affairs. The spiritual, political, and social framework of Spanish government and society was rent asunder early in the nineteenth century. The reputation for individualism and rebelliousness which Spanish people enjoy is presumably due to the great difficulties encountered since that time in developing a sense of unity or cooperation among the various groups into which recent Spanish society has been divided. Individual Spaniards tend to conform rather broadly to the norms of their subgroup, but since the population has been separated into a series of discrete, potentially antagonistic subgroups—or "water-tight compartments," as Ortega y Gasset called them—the modern history of Spain has seen mobs of outer-directed, subgroup-conforming Spaniards locked in bitter rivalry with competing groups. The

74

very absence of creative individualism, of independent objective analysis, has made it difficult for subgroup conformists to see beyond their circle—and the rival group diametrically opposed to it—to develop any sense of the needs and frustrations of Spanish society as a whole.

In the years before the Civil War, the urban and rural proletariats, like the property-owning bourgeois, tended more and more to form closed cultural subgroups, mindful only of their own standards and goals. Lack of identity between working- and middle-class people became accepted almost as axiomatic, and the end result of struggle between closed caste-like groups was considered by many to be the total elimination of the power and interests of one or the other. In many parts of Spain, the triumph of the Nationalists was seen as the victory of "respectable people" over the "rabble." Though Falangist propaganda promised to advance the interests of the lower classes, there was a rather widespread feeling that the latter had been "put in their place."

There is little evidence that the nominally national syndicalist structure of the regime enjoyed much success in transcending the closed, hostile attitude of most working-class people during the 1940's. In the early years of the regime, economic and political realities only reinforced it. Syndicate leaders were appointed from above; and, even after elections were permitted, the general attitude was that anything coming from or connected with the "other side" was a fraud.

The 1940's were not merely a time of social problems and depressed living standards for the working classes alone. General economic prostration and rapid price increases also made life increasingly difficult for the middle classes, most of whom had supported the Nationalists during the Civil War. Throughout that decade, many important articles could only be acquired in adequate quantity on the country's flourishing black market. In coping with this situation, a certain amount of change took place in the composition of the lower middle classes. Persons who had supported the Republic or could not deal with the new economic pressures sometimes went under, to be replaced by those who had made good on the black market. A smaller number of skilled workers, especially among those who had the "good fortune" to be pressed into service on the winning side in the war, managed to elevate themselves into the middle classes.

In one important respect, the regime had no interest in trying to overcome caste division, for if the middle classes should cease to fear the "Red menace" from below, there would be little justification for maintaining the present dictatorial structure. On the other hand, the government had to seek at the very least to de-fuse the antagonism of the lower classes in order to reduce the degree of opposition to workable limits. In certain respects, the regime strove to keep alive a sense of unity among the victors, with a hatred of the "anti-Spain," "Communist subversion" and the ever-present possibility of reversion to revolutionary chaos. But in other ways, it endeavored to de-politicize the workers as well as the middle classes, depriving them of political stimuli other than the official ideology of national solidarity and the syndicalist semi-welfare state. Government demagogy about economic improvements for the workers remained meaningless throughout the 1940's; but, after conditions began to improve during the following decade, it was possible to increase tangible benefits. For the workers, there were rewards for good behavior and punishment for rebellion.

The sullenness of the 1940's eventually gave way to a sense of greater well-being. Improved economic conditions made it possible for middle-class elements to re-establish and often advance their status. The stability of the regime, the efficiency of its police, and its apparent ability to provide a certain amount of bread-and-circuses with security—all discouraged thought about politics and serious matters. By the 1950's, the Spanish middle classes were approaching the patterns of consumer goods fixation, economic striving, and apoliticism that characterized their peers in most other Western countries.

More surprising was the fact that much the same could be said about the workers. The combination of repression, demagogy, and increased opportunity was slowly breaking down the rigid class sense of the 1930's. The very fact of living in an atmosphere free of the incendiary agitation of that earlier decade left the lower classes in a somewhat more tractable mood, and the knowledge that outright social rebellion would probably accomplish nothing also encouraged amenability. But at least as influential as anything else was the opportunity that was being glimpsed by the more skilled workers in the 1950's of escaping abject proletarian economic status.

Admittedly it is more difficult to measure the differences between the real income of Spanish social and economic groups. The Falangist organ *Arriba* observed in 1960 that the upper 14 percent of the population enjoyed 42.5 percent of the national income—an indication of disproportion, though not so extreme as many critics claimed and no worse than in most countries at Spain's level of development. One study, made by the economist Román Perpiñá Grau in 1962, found it possible to divide Spanish families by income groups (see Table 16). These figures, insofar

TABLE 16

Approximate number of families	Approximate percentage of total population	Approximate income
100,000	1.5	$5,000 or more
1,000,000	15	$1,661–$4,800
1,800,000	27	$1,001–$1,660
1,800,000	27	$500–$1,000
1,960,000	29	$500 or less

as they may be accurate, do not so much represent greater equality of income since the Civil War as they do a general increase in all-around income levels.

In 1959, the Chambers of Commerce of Spain undertook a study that showed that, between 1936 and 1958, the price level had increased 12.3 times while the wage level had risen only 5.38 times. If, however, the standard of living had dropped by as much as those figures seemed to indicate, one-third of the population would already have been dead of hunger. What that sort of statistic overlooks are the social benefits and subsidies that are added to wages under the existing syndical contracts and the practice developed by many urban workers of holding two or even three jobs. Some of the benefits are minimal—as late as 1965, old age pensions amounted to only $4.20 per month—but other aspects are more generous. By the late 1950's and 1960's, at least half the population was covered by the full scope of the social security system, providing subsidies for marriages, births, and deaths, unemployment compensation equal to 75 percent of base pay, disability benefits, limited credit facilities, and a wide range of free medical care, which was especially effective in the larger towns. Furthermore, it should be understood that in many cases Spanish salaries are not calculated on the basis of full-time—or at least full-output—work and that there are a large number of paid holidays. By the 1950's it was very easy for skilled and semi-skilled workers to get after-hours jobs in most of the larger cities. Electricians, plumbers, even carpenters, sometimes earned more for three hours labor on special jobs in the evening—not covered by the official low wage scales—than for their more dawdling regular employment in the daytime. The result was a very long work week, probably the longest in western Europe; but, in this way, working-class families were able not merely to get along but to increase significantly their standard of living. A significant minority concentrated more and more upon strictly economic improvement. The goal was to buy a cheap radio, a good suit, and shoes for Sunday, and, if a small automobile was impossible, at least an Italian-model motor scooter. Old proletarian militants shook their heads sadly at these signs of materialistic *embourgeoisement*.

After two decades, the regime finally began to make a significant effort to deal with the urban housing shortage, which grew acute with the startling increase in urban population. During the 1940's, little was done; and, at the end of that decade, the shortage was probably worse than at the close of the Civil War. It was not until the later 1950's that significant improvement was made, as the Ministry of Housing's own figures in Table 17 show.

TABLE 17

Year	Number of entirely or partially government-financed apartments built	
1951	30,985	
1952	34,497	(These figures exclude private
1953	36,502	dwellings built completely
1954	47,467	without government aid. Such
1955	57,898	housing is almost exclusively
1956	73,141	designed for the middle and
1957	75,203	upper classes, and averages
1958	77,064	between 10 and 15 percent of
1959	111,838	the totals given here.)
1960	127,842	

Since 1960, construction has increased rapidly. In 1963, for example, the Ministry of Housing claimed to have supported the building of 206,600 new apartments. At any rate, construction had finally surged well ahead of the rate of urban growth; and, though the housing problem had by no means been solved, the most serious shortages were being eased.

Another indication of higher income is the increased spending on popular amusements—an increase both in absolute volume

D

and in the proportion of expenditures devoted to entertainment. Motion picture-going accounts for some 60 percent of the total amusement receipts, but a major rival appeared in the sports craze that swept the country in the 1950's. Traditionally, Spanish society has had little interest in sports. Track and soccer began to attract attention in the 1920's, only to be partially submerged by the grimmer concerns of the succeeding decade. By mid-century, with political outlets closed and more money available, interest in organized sports, especially soccer (*fútbol*), increased greatly. Soccer matches in the larger towns began to outdraw bullfights several times over. The newly constructed Madrid soccer stadium, Santiago Bernabéu, was one of the largest in the world. Spanish teams won the European championship several times, and Madrid was one of the few cities of the globe to enjoy a daily newspaper, *Marca*, devoted entirely to sports. There was so much attention that political critics charged the regime's censors forced newspapers to devote at least one page per day to sports under penalty of fine. In fact, the government has done relatively little to promote organized sports, which still have scant place in the formal Spanish educational curriculum. Enthusiasm for sports has been, for the most part, a natural, spontaneous development among the ordinary population.

There can be no doubt that the nutrition and medical care of the Spanish people increased significantly in the 1950's and 1960's. Conspicuous consumption by the upper classes is more noticeable than gains in workers' diet, and some observers would more easily credit an *Hoja del Lunes* announcement that some 600,000 bottles of champagne were consumed in the greater Madrid area during the 1965 Christmas holidays than accept official health statistics. Nevertheless, indices from various departments and institutions support each other.

Mortality statistics have shown a gratifying improvement, with the infant mortality rate declining markedly:

1931–35	11.26	1949	6.89
1936–39	12.24	1950	6.42
1940	10.87	1951	6.26
1941	14.29	1952	5.47
1942	10.32	1953	5.28
1943	9.92	1954	4.92
1944	9.30	1955	5.09
1945	8.49	1956	4.64
1946	8.72	1957	4.72
1947	7.07	1958	4.19
1948	6.43	1959	4.11

SOURCE: *Anuario Estadístico 1960.*

In subsequent years, the improvement has continued; and the general death rate has decreased until, for the first time in modern Spanish history, statistics for longevity compare favorably with the rest of western Europe. For males, the average life-span has become about one year longer than in the United States.

Another example of improved physical well-being is shown by the greater height of the younger generation. Army records show that the average height of new recruits in 1955 was 166.08 centimeters, or about 5 feet 5½ inches, a definite increase over pre-Civil War figures, and by 1965 had risen to 167.61 centimeters—approximately 5 feet 6 inches.

The changes that have been mentioned were carried out amid an expanding population. The Civil War had no severe demographic effects on Spain, which in itself may disprove the old legend of "one million killed." The total population, which stood at approximately 25 million in 1935, has increased at a reasonably rapid rate:

1940	25,877,971
1950	27,976,755
1960	30,128,056

This expansion, while vigorous by West European norms, is well below world standards. Maintenance of a moderate rate of growth that offers a broader market on the one hand while avoiding a "population explosion" on the other has probably been a factor in the economic progress of the past two decades.

That the birth rate has remained at a fairly reasonable level—approximately 21.5 live births per thousand population per year in the 1960's—has probably been due to a variety of social and economic factors. Contraception is apparently still not practiced as widely in Spain as in much of western Europe, but the marriage rate is lower and the average age of marriage higher than in any other Western country except Ireland. It is not merely that lower per capita income requires a longer period of work and saving before marriage than is the case in more prosperous countries, for in Portugal, where per capita income is distinctly less than in Spain, there seems also to be less tendency to postpone marriage. Of commensurate importance are the growing pressures of *embourgeoisement*, which raise ambitions and discourage early marriage. In a more genuinely backward country—such as Portugal, in fact, is—these pressures are not so great. Moreover, the vaunted Spanish family structure still remains more cohesive than is the case in some other Western countries. This means less pressure on individuals to have to make their completely independent way in the world and less individual need for marriage for lack of social or familial alternatives. Divorce remains extremely rare, even more so than in certain other Catholic countries, and this requires more careful consideration of initial marriage plans. Another feature of Spanish family patterns is that, as a result of these and other pressures, the birth rate is rather higher among the upper classes than in the urban sectors of the lower classes.

During the first decade after the Civil War, opportunities for emigration were few and did not open up until about 1949, when nearly 42,000 Spaniards moved abroad, mostly to Venezuela. The

"Venezuelan phase" of Spanish emigration lasted until approximately 1955. For the next four years, there was a steady decline in emigration until the widening of the European labor market in 1959–60. Altogether, net emigration during the 1950's amounted to 588,729, and temporary emigration to neighboring countries has proceeded at an even higher rate in the 1960's.

As indicated previously, the sector of Spanish society that has borne the heaviest pressure during the past quarter-century and more is the rural population. This should not be seen as an exclusively Spanish problem, but rather as the Spanish aspect of the common modern dilemma of transforming a largely agrarian society into a predominantly urban, industrial community. The problem is most extreme among the landless proletariat of the south, until recently little affected by most of the meliorative influences of the cities. This group of permanently undernourished, marginally employed farm workers constituted the "Red peasantry" par excellence, and its radicalism was a major factor in bringing on the Civil War. Yet the factors that had provoked its outbursts in the past—ignorance, misery, hopelessness, lack of political leverage—combined with the influence of the landlord class, meant it would continue to receive scant attention for nearly a quarter-century after the Civil War. The urban workers, for better or worse, constituted a visible pressure group that could not be ignored by the regime, but it was much easier to forget about farm laborers. For the most part, they were left out of the state syndical organizations, and so lost the minor advantages in bargaining and fringe benefits which the latter convey to their members. The stagnation of the rural proletariat's social and economic situation is shown by wage and price comparisons in Table 18.

When it is remembered that the original level of 1935 was judged by most impartial observers to be virtually "subhuman," certainly sub-Western, then it can be understood more fully what prolonged misery the continued stagnation of the rural proletariat

TABLE. 18

Year	Index of farm laborers' salaries	General price index	Index of farm laborers' well-being
1935	100	100	100
1942	229.2	247.4	92.6
1945	275.1	274.8	100.1
1950	440.8	529.3	83.2
1955	591	607.5	97.2
1956	643.1	643.1	99.9

SOURCE: Instituto Nacional de Estadística.

has meant. Left to the vagaries of the weather, the market, and the scant social conscience of the large landowners, farm laborers have had little alternative for relief other than migration. As previously indicated, the movement to the cities assumed massive proportions by the 1950's, but the high rural birth rate and the moderate trend toward rural mechanization helped to maintain much of the demographic and economic pressure in the countryside.

During the spring of 1961, Franco made a tour of the southern provinces and, whether or not by design, happened to be shown a few examples of the wretchedness of the rural proletariat. He was said to be genuinely shocked and concerned. This is not very easy to believe, but be that as it may, the growing economic potential of Spain in the 1960's has made it possible to take certain measures to assist farm workers. The new minimum wage legislation of 1963 brought the income of the most poorly paid up to one dollar per day, and new social measures of 1966 were designed to bring the equivalent of much of the urban welfare system to the countryside for the first time. The rural proletariat, nevertheless, still remains the country's principal underprivileged subclass.

In addition to vertical class cleavages, horizontal divisions still persist in the separate regional identifications of the two most productive areas of the country, Catalonia and the Basque provinces. Regional "separatism" was one of the major splits that provoked the Civil War. Catalonia and the Basque country were probably the only general regions where the bulk of the middle classes remained in uneasy association with the proletarian groups to support the Popular Front regime. This generalization, however, must be qualified by significant exceptions among the more conservative and/or wealthy strata of the Basque and Catalan middle classes. Modern political regionalism in Spain has been largely a middle-class phenomenon, and those middle-class elements that felt it necessary to reject ultra-regionalism because of class cleavage during the Civil War soon resumed their regional identification once peace and security returned. The intolerant ultra-centralist policies of the Franco regime soon alienated many middle- and upper-class people in Catalonia who had sided with the Nationalists while the fighting lasted.

The fact that the northeastern districts have largely maintained their industrial lead over the rest of Spain, together with their distinctly higher per capita income, has been important in maintaining a sense of unique regional indentification. The seven provinces of the Basque country and Catalonia contain approximately 16.5 percent of Spain's total population, but account for 25 percent of the national product. In the two Basque provinces of Vizcaya and Guipuzcoa, per capita income is twice the general Spanish norm.

In Catalonia, where regional feeling is most widespread, the survival of the Catalan vernacular as the common domestic language of the bulk of the original population, compounded with the regime's persecution of Catalan culture and education, is perhaps equally important. The easing of controls in the 1950's made it possible for cultural activity in the vernacular to be resumed, though regular education in Catalan is still forbidden. In the Basque country, on the other hand, use of the archaic vernacular is slowly receding. The difficulty and cultural limitations of Basque, which only emerged as a written language in the nineteenth century, have made this non-Indo-European tongue much less viable in preserving an independent cultural ethos and perhaps explains in part why regional feeling is at least somewhat less widespread, if no less militant, in the Basque country.

Other aspects of the social pattern tend to underline Basque and Catalan distinctiveness. Agrarian income and property are more evenly distributed in these two regions than in most parts of the country. The local rural population tends to be more homogeneous and "middle-class" in ethos, fostering a greater sense of stability and solidarity. Religious feeling and participation are more intense in both regions than is the Spanish norm, though the Basques rank well ahead of the Catalans in this regard, evidently because of the tradition of lower-class anti-clericalism and the larger number of unskilled immigrants in the Barcelona-Tarragona area than in the Basque country. According to relative statistics, a disproportionate number of the Spanish clergy come from the Basque country and, to a lesser extent, from Catalonia. Further, proportionate membership in voluntary private associations is much higher in these two regions than in the rest of Spain. According to verifiable statistics, there is even greater interest and participation in sports in Catalonia and the Basque country. Thus, it has been very easy for Basques and Catalans, according to their own lights, to consider themselves: (a) more hard-working, efficient, and productive; (b) more socially and culturally active; (c) more moral and religious; and (d) more generally "modern" and "progressive" than the rest of Spaniards. That there are a number of contradictory aspects to life in these regions or that regionalist opinion sometimes exaggerates local virtues does not alter the fact that such attitudes still broadly persist. Even immigrants from southern Spain tend to become "Catalanized" after a decade in Barcelona. They take pride in participating in a more active society and in enjoying a higher standard of living, and they tend to adopt the commonly critical attitude toward Madrid's corruption, inefficiency, and "exploitation" of Catalonia, since the wealthier Basques and Catalans naturally pay a somewhat larger proportion of the country's taxes. It is not yet altogether clear that the current differential rates of regional social and economic development serve to diminish, rather than to augment, these feelings of separate regional identity and cultural superiority.

Perhaps the most important single change in institutional influence within Spanish society since the beginning of the Civil War has been the increased status of the Catholic Church, which commands greater prestige not merely among the upper and middle classes but to some extent among the lower classes as well. The "residue" of Catholic sentiment among the middle classes and northern peasantry was greater than anti-clericals had thought. This spirit, reawakened by intolerant anti-clericalism and associated with the defense of social and economic status as well as national tradition, provided the principal moral incentive behind the Nationalist effort in the Civil War.

Increasingly during the hundred years prior to that conflict, Spanish Catholicism had become a sort of "class-religion," over-identified with the possessing elements and of less and less concern to the proletariat, urban or rural. In the generation preceding the Civil War, at least a few of the most sensitive leaders in the Church had become concerned about the desiccated quality of religious participation even among the middle classes. The sudden explosion of religious enthusiasm among Nationalists in 1936–37 surprised and overjoyed the ecclesiastical hierarchy, which supposed it the prelude to a genuine spiritual revival. The Church leadership chose to overlook the extent to which this "religious rebirth" was associated with narrow political and social interests. The aftermath revealed the situation in a starker light, and Archbishop Cardinal Gomá, Primate of the Spanish Church and somewhat less given to self-deception than certain of his colleagues, told the British ambassador (also a Catholic) in July 1940 that "contrary to his fervent hopes there had been no real religious revival in Spain since the Civil War." *

And yet the truth of the matter seems to lie somewhere between the effusions of official propaganda and this pessimistic observation by Cardinal Gomá during the last part of his life. The greatly increased prominence of Catholicism in cultural and social activities, the revival of Church education, the rise in religious attendance—all these omnipresent signs of the role and influence of the Church in Franco's Spain are not solely the consequence of the hierarchy's connubium with the dictatorship. Obviously, many middle-class people do associate the belief in and authority of the Catholic Church with the security of the established order, but this is not purely a matter of political and economic motivation. The harsh challenge of the Civil War made a good many of those previously lackadaisical in religious concern more aware of the uncertainties—physical and spiritual— of twentieth-century secularism. Since then, there has been greater appreciation, at least among some, of the need for the moral and spiritual roots that they find in organized religion. Even among the lower classes, the Catholic Church has apparently regained some ground. Though it would be an exaggeration to call the Spanish proletariat of the 1960's "religious," the minority of those who attend mass from time to time seems proportionately slightly greater than in the 1930's. The decline of active anti-clerical sentiment is no doubt due, in large part, to censorship, police repression, and the quasi-monopoly of proselytization facilities by the Church; but it may also, to some

* Sir Samuel Hoare, *Complacent Dictator* (New York, 1947), p. 293.

slight degree, reflect the reorientation of working-class concerns in a more practical direction.

The dictatorship enjoyed the political and religious endorsement of the hierarchy informally from the beginning of the Civil War and officially from July 1937 on. By 1938, it had restored all the religious privileges and perquisites done away with by the Republic and in some respects had gone even further than that. Three years later, Franco arrived at an agreement with the Vatican, which gave him ultimate supervision over the nomination of new members of the hierarchy, the privilege enjoyed by the Crown under the old Concordat. Despite this close association, an official new concordat was not worked out until the last years of Pius XII, in 1953. It ratified existing terms of appointment to the Spanish hierarchy, whereby, for each vacancy, the government suggested six candidates to the Vatican, which selected three, leaving the final choice to the regime. Special preferential jurisdiction was also established for Spanish ecclesiastical problems. Formalizing the relationship of the regime to the Papacy was of political benefit to the former; but, in return, Franco's government further increased the privileges of the Spanish Church. Its supervision of the content of education was recognized, and further media of proselytization and propaganda were placed at its disposal at state expense. In addition to ratifying the existing government obligation to pay clerical salaries and underwrite religious education, the regime also resumed nominal interest payments on the Church properties that had been confiscated an entire century earlier.

The official relationship between Church and state in Spain, together with the ultra-conservative attitude of much of the hierarchy and some of the most conspicuous laity, tends to support the charge of extreme conformism already mentioned. The highly publicized activities of members of the elite Opus Dei group, determined to expand conservative Catholic influence in politics, economics, and education, is yet another clear example of the intimate association of Catholic influence with the power structure of Franco Spain.

Yet there are also examples of Catholic dissidence and of concern to reach out to the lower classes in society as well. Admittedly, the dissidence has on occasion come from the extreme right—as in the celebrated case of Cardinal Segura, former Archbishop of Seville, who denounced the Falange as an instrument of materialistic totalitarianism, yet at the same time demanded tighter moral censorship and the absolute elimination of all Protestantism in Spain. He denounced the 1953 agreement with the liberal, "relativist" United States as godless backsliding—the selling of the national birthright for a mess of potage. Segura may have been against fascist totalitarianism, but he was all for Catholic totalitarianism. The regime eventually arranged with the Vatican for his retirement.

Other less colorful Church leaders, however, have occasionally spoken in a more progressive vein in favor of increased concern for the social and economic problems of the lower classes. The major effort to establish a social reform nexus with the workers, reviving the abortive attempts of members of the previous generation to build a Catholic syndicalism, has been the creation of the HOAC groups (Hermandades Obreras de Acción Católica—Workers' Brotherhoods of Catholic Action). The HOAC organizations, like the "free syndicate" groups that will be described in the last chapter, were organized during the 1950's largely within or under, but nevertheless apart from, the official state syndicates that nominally represent most of the working class. The government's syndical system was never really accepted by the workers, and the official syndicates have much of the time been hollow shells. Small numbers of progressive-minded leaders of the Catholic Action laity attempted to take up the slack by forming small independent groups, whose twin standards were to be economic improvement and Catholic piety. Clerical conservatives have charged that they were mainly just interested in the former concern, while leftist critics denounced them as a clerical fraud. Nevertheless, the HOAC groups by 1960 may have organized as many as 50,000 workers. They were vigorous in their denunciation of social abuses and sometimes stood shoulder to shoulder with leftists in illegal strike maneuvers for higher wages.

Moreover, by 1960, the official leadership of the Church was taking greater pains than in earlier years to avoid automatic identification with the political regime. Franco's advancing age and the possibility of renewed leftist and anti-clerical opposition prompted greater care for the future. A number of letters from high Church leaders were released indirectly, protesting against specific abuses, especially the arrest of HOAC leaders or persecution of HOAC affiliates. Further, after generations of silence, the hierarchy rediscovered the farm laborer. It is surprising that this took so long, for the indifference to religion is greatest in the rural southern provinces, such as Huelva and Cordoba, where it appears that those who have nothing at all to do with the Church number half the population—a higher proportion than even in proletarian industrial areas. In 1965, one southern prelate spoke out formally to denounce the abject misery of the rural laborers and encourage the regime's belated palliatives.

The situation of Spanish Protestantism has been the exact reverse of that of the Catholic Church. The small Protestant minority, no more than 30,000 out of a population of 25 million at the end of the Civil War, has been denied legal identity, persecuted in almost every conceivable way, and, in the early years of the regime, seemed in danger of physical elimination. Protestant educational and proselytization facilities have been prohibited, Protestant congregations have been denied the right to own and administer church buildings or even to identify their places of worship. Yet, in spite of both official and informal

persecution, the Spanish Protestant community has expanded
under the Franco regime, nearly doubling its numbers within
thirty years. There is a distinct difference in tone and quality
between Catholicism and Protestantism in Spain. To want to be
a Protestant, one must indeed take religion seriously, while the
Spanish Catholic Church still counts among its nominal adherents
literally millions of people who have almost nothing to do with
church services or religious practice.

The regime's persecution of Protestantism has long been a
talking point for liberal critics abroad, mainly in Protestant
countries. Accordingly, the most recent phase in the regime's
perpetual mock-liberalization program brought a change in religious laws permitting Protestants somewhat greater freedom of
activity. Though the move has correctly been interpreted as
merely another public relations ploy, it has brought the customary howls of anguish from what some Spanish commentators
call sarcastically the "super-Catholics."

Any brief analysis of social change in Franco's Spain must
finally take into consideration the most important professional
subsector within the country, the Army officer corps. The role of
the military in modern Spain has been of vital significance, not
because of any greater wisdom or technical development which
Army officers have acquired, but because they ultimately em-
body organized force capable of deciding the issue in national
crises—of which Spain has had quite a number in the past one
hundred fifty years. As far as social background and ordinary
routine are concerned, the Army officer corps might be characterized as a special example of middle-class bureaucracy. Officers
have never had a distinctly defined social and political ideology,
other than vaguely defined allegiances to "service," "the fatherland," and "progress." Partly because of this, their role in the
major social and political conflicts of modern Spain has often
been uncertain. Had it not been for the lack of well-structured
political order in the country, almost all of them would have pre-

ferred not to face any responsibility other than their professional duties.

Before the profound cleavage that divided Spanish society in 1936, the only group able to react effectively against the Popular Front was the Army. After many sections of the Army rose in revolt, the military were passionately criticized by all leftist commentators for having dared to take independent responsibility for the national political dilemma. In an earlier chapter, it has been explained how the Franco regime began as a rather rudimentary military dictatorship, though it soon achieved more sophisticated organization. One of the political paradoxes of Franco's government has been that a regime that was originated by military rebellion should have had so little difficulty avoiding potential rebelliousness by the military. Insofar as the career attitude of the great majority of officers is concerned, the Franco dictatorship has succeeded where the Republic failed in encouraging a more strictly professional attitude than has been seen among the Spanish military in quite some time. Since there has been no political breakdown or crisis to prompt military intervention, Army officers largely have been able to avoid politics altogether, except among the senior hierarchy.

Since the early 1950's, professionalization of military life has proceeded apace. New and more effective training programs, modernized equipment, technical assistance from the United States, have all encouraged this trend. Indeed, the major discontent shown by Army officers in recent years has not concerned military dissidence, but lingering professional frustration. Officer salaries remain low, and it is still almost impossible to support a family on a lieutenant's income. Despite recent improvements, materiél and training are still not quite up to the standards of the best Western forces. The significant thing is that it is on these areas that ordinary officers concentrate their attention, not upon the political vacuum that exists in Spain. So long as the regime cares for its own problems, Army officers are not interested in developing a political vocation. Thus, where leftists in the 1930's criticized much of the Army for trying to fulfill a concept of positive civic responsibility, the opposition of the 1960's tends to disparage the military for having "no ideology," for showing no interest in political affairs, but concentrating almost exclusively on its professional role.

5 / Cultural Affairs

Literary historians sometimes speak of the two generations preceding the Civil War as a "Silver Age" of Spanish writing, second only to the high period of Cervantes and Calderón. In the graphic arts, names such as Picasso, Miró, Gris, and Dalí testify to fundamental Spanish contributions to the esthetic forms of the twentieth century. There were also significant achievements in some of the social and natural sciences, as evidenced in the work of the historian Rafael Altamira, the philologist Ramón Menéndez Pidal, and the biologist Ramón y Cajal. Spanish intellectuals may sometimes exaggerate, in nostalgic retrospect, the accomplishments of the pre-Civil War generation, but there seems little doubt it brought Spanish culture nearer the level of modern Europe than any of its predecessors.

In no realm of endeavor were the consequences of the Civil War more destructive than in cultural affairs. Conditions of total civil war and ideological absolutism precluded the work of genuine intellectuals on either side, and the resultant emigration involved a disproportionate share of the country's cultural elite. The great majority of Spanish intellectuals who have won international attention since the Civil War have been among the émigré group: the Nobel prize-winning poet Juan Ramón Jiménez, the Nobel prize-winning biochemist Severo Ochoa, the cellist

Pau Casals, the novelist Ramón Sender, the writer Salvador de Madariaga, the medievalists Américo Castro and Claudio Sánchez Albornoz. Not all the intellectuals who have emigrated have done so for political reasons; many are attracted simply by the greater rewards and opportunities found elsewhere.

For the opposition, the cultural policy of the Franco regime has been epitomized by the hyperbolic remarks attributed to General Millán Astray at Salamanca in 1936, when the Nationalist propaganda chief was supposed to have shouted at Unamuno, "¡Viva la muerte! Muerta la inteligencia!" ("Long live death! Death to the intelligence!") The situation has not in fact been that radical, but neither has it permitted any large measure of freedom or stimulated genuine creativity. The cultural policy of the regime might be labeled authoritarian Catholic neo-conservatism, based on state censorship and direction.

Three main attitudes may be discerned among the pro-Nationalist cultural elite during the Civil War: (a) Catholic conservatism, anti-liberal, anti-individualist, stressing the primacy of religious values, usually monarchist in politics and determined to destroy the laic influence of the Republic; (b) Falangist nationalism, also anti-liberal and anti-individualist, nominally Catholic in religion, but both anti-clerical and anti-monarchist politically, eager to create a new nationalist, elitist culture based on modernized Spanish values, harmonizing tradition with the revolutionary demands of the twentieth century; and (c) elements of pragmatic conservatism, little interested in culture as such, supporters of Catholic orthodoxy in the interest of unity and security, advocates of censorship to discourage subversive ideas, but willing to encourage certain kinds of technological development provided it did not cost much money. The regime's education laws, written in 1938, were drawn up largely to the specifications of Catholic conservatism, with the Church given authority to regulate and censor the content of secular as well as clerical education. The major terms of the preceding Concordat were honored, the state paying most of the cost of Catholic educational activities. Protestant evangelical work, which operated with complete freedom during the five years of the Republic for the only time in Spanish history, once more was sharply curtailed.

The new "Falangist intelligentsia" consisted of a relatively small number of individuals, led by a few luminaries such as the Catalan writer Eugenio d'Ors, the essayist Pedro Laín Entralgo, and the neo-classical poet Dionisio Ridruejo. The notion of a new elitist culture that they tried to project was, as Ridruejo and others have since admitted, vague, confused, and immature. It was compounded of nostalgic romanticism and fascistic irrationality, but aimed at saving certain elements of the heritage of the generation of 1898 and of Ortega, rather than rejecting this *in toto* as did the clerical conservatives. Though the regime's first regular Minister of Education was the monarchist clerical Pedro Sáinz Rodríguez, control of state propaganda was later given to young Falangists such as Ridruejo and the philologist Antonio Tovar. Their task was to propagate the ideology of Franquist national syndicalism, to channel cultural activity along nationalist, anti-liberal lines, and, by their own standards, to foster a new elitist, dynamically Hispanic pattern of cultural expression. Yet their Falangist cultural ideas did not have broad support in the Nationalist movement; and, after the downfall of Serrano Súñer, their places were filled by more conservative officials. During the Civil War and the following decade, the Falangist intellectuals founded a number of shortlived cultural reviews—*Jerarquía, Vértice, Escorial, Alcalá, Tajo,* and *Sí*—but all failed for lack of support. By the late 1940's, "cultural Falangism" was practically dead. Much of its stimulus had been derived from the international vogue of the '30's, cut short by the end of the European war. Ridruejo rejected the regime and passed over to the opposition, while others withdrew into private life. Those Falangist ideologues remaining in the government were used to grind out propaganda that sometimes had little to do with the original doctrines of Falangism.

The ideological brain trust at the end of the Civil War was the recently founded Instituto de Estudios Políticos, charged with the study of political and social science and pre-legislative research. Rather than acting as the preserve of orthodox fascistic Falangism, the IEP and its directors soon became responsible for the ideological rationalization of the unending tactical shifts of the regime. Already by 1942, the concept of "totalitarianism" was being criticized, laying the doctrinal groundwork for the subsequent phase of de-fascistization. Further changes occurred during the long tenure of Francisco Javier Conde (1948–57). An ex-Socialist and former law professor, Conde was a talented ideological tactician who had begun his career under the regime by trying to formulate a sociological and juridical theory of caudillaje in justification of dictatorship. He later tried to stress the evolutionary, "social-minded" characteristics of the regime, hoping to make Franco's national syndicalism more palatable to West European democracy. In recent years the IEP has been confined to a largely academic role, but serves as an important nexus with political and social science studies in other countries.

Another phase of cultural liberalization was attempted by Joaquín Ruiz Jiménez, who served as Minister of Education from 1951 to 1956. A Catholic moderate, Ruiz Jiménez was chosen to succeed a Catholic ultra-conservative in the first major cabinet realignment after the Franco regime had been accepted by the non-Communist West. Although Ruiz Jiménez did not initiate broad changes in educational policy as a whole, he tried to accelerate educational development and, more visibly, to liberalize the tone of higher education, encouraging semi-public dialogue between "liberal Catholic" and "left Falangist" intellectuals. In the process, he was bitterly criticized in ultra-conservative circles and was blamed indirectly for the incidents at the University of Madrid in 1956. Perhaps the principal achievement of Ruiz Jiménez's tenure was to admit a little fresh air in the hitherto stifling climate of ideological discussion. After leaving the government, he himself later passed over into the ranks of the moderate opposition as editor of *Cuadernos para el Diálogo*, a politico-cultural journal supported by open-minded Catholics.

The range of intellectual discussion was ultimately determined by the state censorship, long under the direction of the Catholic ultra, Gabriel Arias Salgado, through his post as Vice-Secretary of Popular Education and later as Minister of Information. A Galician by birth, Arias was credited with having lifelong connections with Franco. He had once been a seminary student; and, though unable to continue a clerical vocation, he enjoyed two decades of sweeping power as cultural and educational arbiter. Certain kinds of publications, such as intra-university journals, were free from the scrutiny of the agents of this frustrate Torquemada, but all ordinary literature, educational material, social science, and humanist studies and all newspapers except Church organs felt his heavy hand. Though probably the most hated man in Spain among the intelligentsia, Arias Salgado's repressive zeal never slackened. During the last years of his long tour of duty, he was said to have become increasingly concerned even about such matters as the kind of music played on the National Radio during the evening.

Nowhere has the onus of official censorship been more stultifyingly revealed than in the quality of the Spanish daily press. During the two generations before the Civil War, Spanish newspaper activity had been among the liveliest in the world. Much of the daily press had not been very accurate or responsible, but it had certainly been stimulating. The contrast since the Civil War has been almost absolute. The entire left-wing and liberal press was completely annihilated. A series of official government organs, nominally Falangist, was established in Madrid and the other large cities. Nearly all the conservative papers were allowed to continue, and these have largely dominated the provincial press for the past quarter-century, though under strict prior censorship. The few exceptions are special Catholic publications, such as the hierarchy's official *Ecclesia,* and an occasional enterprise that is willing to test the outer limits of censorship, such as the slightly heterodox Madrid syndicalist daily *Pueblo,* edited by the "left" Falangist Emilio Romero.

Yet another fact as culturally and intellectually debilitating as the dull, narrow, tendentious character of the Spanish press was the problem that, through most of the period of the Franco regime, a sizable minority of the adult population was illiterate. During the Republican years, adult illiteracy was calculated at nearly 25 percent. A major effort was made before the Civil War to build new schools and extend primary education, but a great deal of ground was lost in the decade 1936–45. Exact figures are not available, but probably a smaller percentage of school-age children received formal instruction in the early 1940's than a decade earlier.

Obviously the dilemma of adequate primary education is related in one way or another to many other Spanish problems. From the beginning of the regime, it was also clear that the primary responsibility lay with the central government. Despite the spiritual and censorial tutelage of the Catholic Church, only about 25 percent of the country's elementary education facilities were Church schools. The Ministry of Education long lacked the resources to expand and improve the operation of the three-quarters of Spain's primary schools for which it was responsible. Moreover, literate Falangist party veterans with some sort of accreditation were frequently rewarded after the Civil War with teaching positions, though their pedagogical talent was often questionable. Even more debilitating were the almost impossibly low salaries paid to most teachers, which required many to divert part of their time to supplementary employment. Significant progress was not made until the 1950's. By the end of that decade, some sort of school was available in almost every locality, though small villages and slum districts in the larger cities were still sometimes without facilities. Official statistics in 1960 put the adult illiteracy rate at no more than 13 percent, but such claims are misleading, for it would appear that a great many "functional illiterates" were included in the "literate" 87 percent. Moreover, the provision of nominal facilities says little about the quality of instruction and level of learning, which remain low. In most areas, classrooms have been quite overcrowded and frequently lack equipment.

Though official statistics indicated that as late as 1962 less than two-thirds of the school-age population went as far as the eighth grade, during the preceding decade the number of students enrolled in Spanish secondary schools increased 243 percent, an advance proportionately greater than that in either France or Italy. But Spain was starting from a much lower level and in 1962 had only 240 students in secondary school for every 10,000 inhabitants, compared with 484 in Italy.

Proportionately even more severe than problems of basic education is the paucity of resources for technical education. In a notable attempt to begin to meet the shortage, the Ministry of Labor began in the 1950's a program of building six new "labor universities," or large-scale polytechnic institutes, which would provide advanced professional training in the crafts of modern industry, along with regular university instruction. It was planned that most of the student quota be reserved for sons of state syndicate members, so that the schools would be genuine "proletarian universities." By the end of the decade, six labor universities had been completed at Gijón, La Coruña, Zamora, Seville, Córdoba, and Tarragona, and two more were later begun at Huesca and Cáceres. During the 1960's, a much broader though less intensive "Worker's Promotion Program" was begun, which claimed by 1966 to be operating 150 mobile training centers in various parts of the country, advancing the mechanical skills of several hundred thousand workers. The Ministry of Labor's official statistics seem very promising, but the current production of qualified mechanics and engineers still falls far short of the demand, much less the potential required in the future.

Inadequate though the record has been in primary education and trade schools, the development of the Spanish university system under the regime is no more impressive. The professoriat was thinned by the Civil War emigration and the purge that followed. For the most part chairs are held by men of reliably conservative opinions, though pressure has not been so severe as to preclude the continuing existence of a doughty minority of moderate liberals. As in most European countries with a centralized state university system, the curriculum has remained rather narrow, with studies divided among Faculties of Law, Medicine, Humanities (*Filosofía y Letras*), Science, and Pharmacy. A Faculty of Economics and Political Science was introduced at Madrid in 1943, and Faculties of Economics were later added at three other universities.

The number of students in universities and technical schools doubled between 1940 and 1960, but the great majority, as in most other countries, still come from the upper and middle classes. Those in the newly developed labor universities constitute the principal exception. Moreover, a university degree does not provide automatic entree to a profitable career because of the overconcentration in Law, Medicine, and the Humanities. After reaching an all-time high in 1953, the total number of students of Law has begun to decline and the number specializing in Medicine or Humanities has become stabilized, but the only graduates assured of meaningful employment are the small minority who complete technical training in the sciences.

A major force in higher education by the 1950's was the Opus Dei group, which achieved great influence in certain university departments at the cost of deep resentment among many non-Opus professors. Opus Dei also established a new university all its own, the Estudio General de Navarra, in ultra-conservative, Carlist Pamplona. Though successive Spanish regimes had always resisted pressures to certify a Church university on the same level as the state institutions, Opus leaders pressed for complete certification of their school.

The main effort of the Franco regime to foster intellectual activity and research has been made through the Superior Council of Scientific Investigation (CSIC), which was established under the Ministry of Education in 1939. Since spontaneous support for work in the natural and social sciences has been rarely available in Spain, it attempted to finance a great deal of the country's intellectual endeavor in the depressed atmosphere that followed the Civil War. The CSIC organized a complicated variety of subsections and individual institutes for studies in many different fields. The total support was not great, however; and shortage of funds has proved a severe handicap, especially in the natural and physical sciences.

One sad case in point was that of Spain's leading physicist, Arturo Duperier, who carried on the most fruitful part of his career abroad, helping to develop Britain's atomic bomb. In his old age, he was lured back to Spain by promises that full research facilities would be made available to him in his native country. These guarantees were not fulfilled, and he died amid profound disappointment in 1959.

The situation has improved since then. An able group of young scientists has been collected under the Instituto de Energía Nuclear and is conducting significant new research, partly under subcontract from the United States' Atomic Energy Commission. The Spanish Government's decision not to build its own atomic bomb was prompted more by political discretion than by scientific inadequacy. Yet ordinary Spanish work in the sciences does not measure up to achievements in this particular glamor field, and there still remains the need for large-scale investment and much more advanced training before Spanish laboratories will be able to make significant accomplishments in most aspects of scientific endeavor.

The situation in the social sciences is equally frustrating. There are a few individuals in almost every major social science discipline in Spain who have made outstanding achievements, but they still operate in something of a vacuum. Original work is hampered in some instances by censorship, but perhaps just as much by traditional cultural attitudes and the humanist essay tradition and impressionist tendencies of the liberal intellectuals.

Historical studies have been carried on more successfully, in part because they can be concentrated on earlier periods that do not necessarily raise controversial questions. Not unnaturally, the principal achievements have occurred in the field of medieval history. The outstanding Spanish historian of the 1950's, Jaime Vicens Vives, developed a promising circle of younger historians at the University of Barcelona, devoted to early modern and nineteenth-century studies, as well as medieval topics. Vicens helped turn attention to problems of social and economic change, long ignored in Spanish historical investigation.

Much of the personnel of the country's publishing industry moved to Spanish America during and at the close of the Civil War. The flight of talent, general fatigue, censorship, and an extreme scarcity of paper in the 1940's caused book publication to decline severely, so that Spain has been long in regaining the volume of 1935.

There was a considerable increase in the quantity of literary publication during the 1950's, but the quality was unimpressive. Since the Civil War the Spanish novel has been largely conventional in form and almost completely anodyne in content. The country's literary world long remained impervious to contemporary cultural currents. Prose writing during the Franco era has mostly taken the form of middle-class pseudo-realist narratives, rarely transcending simple storytelling.

The outstanding prose stylist of the contemporary Hispanic world, Camilo José Cela, scored the first post-Civil War success with a brief narrative, *La familia de Pascual Duarte* (1942), which set a vogue of *tremendismo,* blending ingredients of violence, cynicism, and strong (though never obscene) vocabulary. Since then Cela has exhibited his extraordinary stylistic virtuosity in nearly a score of volumes, excelling in the descriptive vignette and in his regional travel books. He has written only two or three works that might genuinely be called novels, for he has few if any ideas and little of serious intent to say about society and human relations. His remarkable linguistic inventiveness and esthetic craftsmanship have earned him wide influence in Spanish letters, though there has also been some tendency for his admirers to ape his deep pessimism and hostile, egocentric attitudes as well.

One unique feature of the post-Civil War literary scene has been the emergence of women novelists in numbers for the first time. A half dozen or more have won prizes, and the best is probably Ana María Matute, whose first major work, *En esta tierra* (1955), revealed a didactic and social dimension uncommon in Spanish literature of those years. Her writing has gone on to develop a distinct personal style and ambience that is at its most effective in several works that re-create the world of childhood.

The best single novel written in Franco's Spain is *El Jarama* (1955), by Rafael Sánchez Ferlosio, son of a leading Falangist intellectual. Its achievement is to reproduce with telling accuracy the conversations and activities of a group of middle-class young people from Madrid on a Sunday excursion. The naturalness of dialogue in this "epic of vulgarity" has rarely been equaled in any literature; and, though the novel is utterly devoid of any explicit meaning, it has stood out among the artificiality of its competitors.

Since the mid-1950's, other purposive examples of literary

endeavor have appeared. The most widely read was José María Gironella's *Los cipreses creen en dios,* a broad if mediocre canvas of society in the Catalan provincial capital of Gerona in the years leading up to the Civil War. It sold especially well in English translation. More recently, the "social novel" has been practiced with skill and some subtlety by Juan Goytisolo, a young leftist who finds life most congenial in French exile.

Work in the theater has been, if anything, more conventional and escapist than in prose fiction. As in most Western countries, middle-class comedies abound. Among the few exceptions are the dramas of two capable playwrights, Antonio Buero Vallejo and Alfonso Sastre, whose writing usually carries didactic overtones and, particularly in the case of Buero, reveals skill in dramatic construction.

No major new figure has appeared in Spanish poetry since the Civil War. Though a considerable amount of verse is written, nearly all of it is either pedestrian, derivative, or characterized by hollow virtuosity.

The quality of recent Spanish painting is more substantial. Spanish artists have preserved traditional forms more than have their Western contemporaries; but this, together with the expression of distinctive personal accents, has sometimes enabled them to produce work with more meaningful content than is common in the mid-twentieth century. Many Spanish painters have also adopted the forms of abstraction that have become trademarks of recent style; and, by about 1960, some of these had begun to draw international attention. Probably the most outstanding has been the Catalan Antoni Tàpies, sometimes called "the black knight of modern painting." His dark, somber, carefully restrained and modulated canvases have presented one of the most unique and individual styles in the abstract expressionism of the past two decades. In addition to the achievements in painting, notable work has also been done in recent decades by Spanish sculptors such as Eduardo Chillida and Pablo Serrano.

The Spanish film industry, which dates back to the 1890's, has expanded in volume since 1939, but the quality of its productions has been mediocre. This has not been for lack of an audience. By 1965, Spain had 7,902 motion picture theaters, a ratio of one for every 5,100 inhabitants, surpassed only by Italy among European countries—and, in the ratio of motion picture seats per number of inhabitants, Spain exceeds Italy. The main obstacle has probably been the competition of the international motion picture industry. The Spanish-speaking world constitutes so vast a market that almost any promising film produced abroad is dubbed in Spanish, creating a vast repertoire difficult to compete with. Only a very few Spanish directors—most notably Juan Bardem—have produced work of quality and originality. The most interesting movie made in Spain in recent years, Luis Buñuel's surrealistic *Viridiana* (1961), which satirizes both "traditional" and "popular" Spain, could be completed only because of a temporary oversight by the censorship. The movie was subsequently banned from exhibition in Spain, and Buñuel returned to the Mexican exile where he had spent most of the past twenty years.

A significant ploy in the "liberalization" of the regime, especially with regard to freedom of expression, was the appointment of the political science professor Manuel Fraga Iribarne as Minister of Information in 1962. Fraga soon promised a new press law permitting greater spontaneity and freedom of speech, but was nearly four years in preparing it. When instituted in April 1966, this measure abolished prior censorship, but left the state with full authority for ex post facto censorship, confiscation, imprisonment, and fines for anything printed that might be judged contrary to "truth," "morality," or the "fundamental laws." The new regulation aimed at achieving self-censorship by news-

papers and presses, all of which were required to deposit copies of their work with the authorities prior to publication. All materials remained liable to confiscation; and editors, if in doubt, were urged to consult the authorities first. After thirty years of dictatorship, Spanish writers and editors were well aware of the bounds of the permissible, and promulgation of the new regulations did not result in any outburst of new criticism. In fact, no significant change in the daily newspapers was noticeable. Writers in various fields had already been taking greater liberties than would have been countenanced in the 1940's, but complete exchange of ideas and unrestrained commentary was still impossible. It seemed likely that this would be the case so long as the basic structure of the regime continued.

6 / The Opposition

Though nearly 300,000 Republicans fled Spain during the closing months of the Civil War, the majority of Republican Army veterans and Popular Front activists remained behind to face the vengeance of their conqueror. Altogether, these categories included by 1939 more than three million so-called "Reds" who had been either members of Socialist or Anarchist unions, participants in the various Popular Front parties, or soldiers in the wartime Republican Army. They amounted to perhaps one-third of the active adult male population.

From the very beginning, the Franco dictatorship faced what it deemed a security problem of massive proportions. The first directives of the military conspiracy of 1936 stressed the difficulty of an active minority establishing control over mass leftist movements and urged swift use of terror, imprisonment, and an unspecified number of executions of leaders to paralyze the opposition. The Civil War subsequently became famous for the gory extent of the "Red" and "White Terrors" on opposing sides. It will not be possible to determine the number of victims of the Nationalist regime until after it comes to an end, and perhaps not even then. Contrasting approaches to calculating the volume of Franco's "White Terror" during the Civil War may be found in the appendices to Gabriel Jackson's *The Spanish Republic and the Civil War* (1965), which holds that it amounted to 200,000, and in Hugh Thomas' widely read *The Spanish Civil War* (1961), which cites different if equally inconclusive evidence to suggest that Nationalist executions were fewer than those of the Popular Front and did not total more than 40,000. Direct proof to substantiate any precise estimate is lacking, though available demographic evidence would seem to support a reasonably moderate figure.

It would appear that the number of political executions by the regime after the Civil War, mainly during the years 1939–43, was considerably greater than during the Civil War itself. Once the conflict closed, the dictatorship had the opposition at its mercy and implemented a "final solution" of social and political prophylaxis on a grand scale. Thousands of Nationalists who had lost close relatives to the gunmen of the Popular Front indulged a passionate lust for vengeance. The simplest sort of denunciation or vague allegation often was enough to bring arrest, severe penalties, and sometimes death. There was a general feeling that prominent leftists or Republicans who had held positions of leadership were incurable and might as well be liquidated. Only those of the rank-and-file who had exercised no initiative were deemed capable of re-education and redemption. The execution policy was further encouraged by the apogee of the fascist regimes on the European continent. In fact, it was the collapse of Fascist Italy and the impending defeat of Nazi Germany that apparently influenced the regime to moderate its procedures—that, plus the fact that by 1943 the leadership cadres of the leftist groups had been completely decimated.

The prison population in the spring of 1939 was enormous, requiring the hasty establishment of rudimentary barbed-wire concentration camps. It stood at the following levels during the regime's early years:

| 1940 | 270,719 | 1942 | 159,392 | 1944 | 74,095 |
| 1941 | 233,373 | 1943 | 124,423 | | |

SOURCE: *Anuario Estadístico 1944–1945*. The figures are for January 1 of each year.

It is impossible to learn exactly how many of these prisoners were executed and how many later amnestied. Eléna de la Souchère, in her *Explication de l'Espagne* (1962), has tried to reach a rough estimate on the basis of the official death statistics, which reveal some 220,000 more fatalities for the three years 1939–41 than for the three years 1933–35. This is not an altogether satisfactory method of computation, since depressed living conditions and poor nutrition and medical care meant that the mortality rate would be higher during those years in any case. In 1941, for example, there were 28,000 more deaths of females than in 1935, but even the regime's bitterest foes would not suggest that it necessarily shot 28,000 women during that year. Since any increase in deaths from natural causes ought presumably to be shared equally among males and females, a more meaningful figure might be that where male deaths exceed female deaths compared with the pre-Civil War ratio where approximately 10,000 more males than females died each year. The male death rate exceeded the female death rate by a total of 145,000 for the four years 1939–42 and did not return to the old balance until about 1947. Likewise, the Instituto Nacional de Estadística shows a total increase of approximately 92,000 "homicides and other violent deaths" for these four years over and above the pre-war averages of about 7,500 per year. A further surplus of 22,000 is recorded for the five years 1943–47. The number of "homicides and other violent deaths" does not begin to approach the pre-war figures until 1948, when it drops to 8,985. The only statistic about political executions that has ever been obtained from a quasi-official source was an undifferenti-

E

ated total of 192,684 for the five years 1939–1944,* but there is no guarantee whatever of its accuracy. At any rate, it does not seem unlikely that, during the decade following the Civil War, the regime may have executed as many as 100,000 former Republican and working-class activists for their responsibilities in Popular Front politics or revolutionary violence. Supporters of the Franco regime argued that such responsibilities were common crimes, forgetting that similar deeds in the name of counter-revolution went unpunished.

By 1939, most supporters of the Popular Front felt themselves beaten. Defeatism was a major factor in the collapse of the Republican effort, and the general war-weariness and frustration assisted the Nationalist takeover of the entire country once the fighting ended. Yet the cleavage was too deep, the emotional identifications too intense, the policy of the victors too vindictive for all the pro-Republican community to be absorbed without protest into the Nationalists' new authoritarian society. A large underground resistance movement existed from the first week of the Republican surrender. The domestic opposition functioned on three levels: clandestine cells of the former political parties, efforts to maintain shadow groupings of workers loyal to the old syndicates apart from the government trade unions, and bands of *guerrilleros* devoted to direct action, usually in the mountainous regions of the country.

Apart from the domestic opposition, there were the surviving members of the Republican Government-in-exile, with head-quarters in Paris until the German occupation. The *émigré* politicians continued to be severely divided by party and faction, just as during the Civil War. Afterwards, the main split was still between the Communists and Communist supporters such as the former premier Juan Negrín, on the one hand, and the anti-Communist majority Socialists and liberals, on the other. There

* Charles Foltz, Jr., *The Masquerade in Spain* (Boston, 1947), p. 97.

were, however, a number of minor splits and rivalries: between the extremist (Largo Caballero) and moderate (Prieto) sectors of the Socialists, between the Socialists and the Anarchists, between the moderate Catalanists and the radical Catalanists, and later even between the moderate and radical Anarchists. Differences in principle and personality hampered the first efforts to provide for the post-war *émigrés*. The Communists and Negrinists set up a "Servicio de Evacuación de Republicanos Españoles" (SERE) to care for their followers among the emigration in France and Mexico. The Socialists under Prieto countered with a "Junta de Auxilio a los Republicanos Españoles" (JARE) to assist the anti-Communist majority.

Once the Civil War ended, however, the activity of official leaders outside Spanish soil was no longer decisive for the opposition struggle inside Spain. It is too early to write the history of the domestic opposition during the first years, for this consisted of a large series of small, clandestine, usually poorly coordinated activities in many parts of Spain. At no time during the period of the Second World War were these sufficiently serious to menace the existence of the dictatorship itself, but the resistance and the accompanying slowdown in economic output were so widespread as to weaken the regime's strength and help discourage adventures in foreign policy. The resistance maintained strong antipathy to the official trade unions among the workers, so that the official syndical structure for long remained an empty artifice imposed on the labor force from above.

Running gunfights with guerrilla bands in the mountains were carried on by the Civil Guards, and on at least a few occasions by the Army, for more than ten years after the Civil War. The first *guerrilleros* probably emerged in the low hills of Galicia in 1936–37, in many cases being leftist militants from the coastal district who had fled the Nationalist wartime draft. Units were formed both in the towns and countryside and carried on minor harassment even during the war. Guerrilla bands were also formed in the mountains of Andalusia, León, and Asturias after the Nationalists occupied those areas. By 1941, the security forces were able to disrupt much of the guerrilla activity, because of improving police skills and because the *guerrilleros* were being deserted by the regular opposition political parties. The latter saw little immediate chance of success in a Europe dominated by Nazi Germany and feared that guerrilla warfare might be doing more harm than good.

Just as the Nationalist victory in the Civil War had been contingent upon German and Italian aid, so the opposition's hope for the overthrow of the regime was predicated upon defeat of the fascist powers in the World War. The main participation of the opposition in the international struggle against fascism came from the large emigration, a quarter-million strong, in France. These refugees had been badly treated by the French authorities —some 70,000 dying within the first three years, according to a Vichy announcement of May 1942. Yet thousands joined the Maquis, and a total of 24,715 served in six brigades of the organized Free French army forces.

So long as most of France either was occupied by German troops or was a potential battleground, it could not be used as an effective staging area for the counteroffensive of leftist forces. The most hospitable center for political *émigrés* was Mexico, where the first new effort at intra-opposition unity was made in 1943, when Socialist and Republican Liberal leaders established a "Junta Española de Liberación." Its weakness was that this remained largely a paper organization of *émigré* leaders and excluded sizable sectors of the opposition, since neither Anarcho-Syndicalists nor Communists participated.

By 1944, the impending defeat of Germany gave great impetus to the Resistance. Clandestine groups stepped up their work as hundreds of young men ran off to join guerrilla bands. In some industrial areas the Anarcho-Syndicalists set up shadow syndicates of their own and claimed to receive token dues from as much as one-third the total labor force in those regions. Police treatment became less rigorous. More and more of the regime's employees showed that they doubted the dictatorship would survive the Second World War and that they wanted to establish credit with the opposition. The underground groups attempted to achieve greater concentration of effort by establishing their own "Alianza Nacional de Fuerzas Democráticas" within Spain on the basis of most of the former Popular Front groups.

Leftist and liberal groups abroad, with the official encouragement of the Soviet Union, demanded that the Allied powers force a change of regime in Spain. To take advantage of the new situation, the Republican Government-in-exile was reactivated in 1945 and afterwards relocated in Paris. Spanish members of the French Resistance, sometimes led by Communists, were organized into guerrilla bands that crossed the Pyrenees to spark wider rebellion. Within parts of northern Spain, there was established a clandestine "Agrupación de Fuerzas Armadas Republicanas Españolas" (AFARE) to try to organize the former members of the wartime Republican Army. A parallel organization of ex-Republican Army officers was set up in France. All the while, diplomatic pressure mounted, leading to the closing of the Pyrenean frontier and the withdrawal of diplomatic representatives from Madrid at the end of 1946.

Spanish Conservatives were anxious to safeguard the future by establishing a more moderate opposition to Franco and were encouraged by D. Juan, son of Alfonso XIII and heir to the throne, whose Lausanne Manifesto of 1945 rejected totalitarianism and espoused constitutional monarchy. During the following year a "Confederación de Fuerzas Monárquicas" was organized of old-line monarchists, clerical conservatives, and moderate Catalan regionalists. To leaders of the Alianza Nacional de Fuerzas Democráticas, it proposed creation of a national anti-Franco front with the aim of holding a democratic plebiscite on the question of restoring the Crown. This would have completely undercut the shadow Republican Government-in-exile. The Anarcho-Syndicalists, who had never supported the liberal parliamentary Republic, were favorably disposed to the monarchist proposal, but it was rejected by the Socialists and other opposition groups.

By the end of 1946, an "Ejército Republicano de Liberación" was nominally established, with an office in Paris directed by the Socialist General José Asenio. The Communist military leaders Enrique Líster and Juan Modesto seem to have been active in this group, some of the most important nuclei of the proposed force being products of a recently established Communist guerrilla school near Toulouse. Related elements also recruited volunteers to fight for the Communists in Greece, arguing that the establishment of a new "democratic" regime in Athens would add support for a Republican government in Spain.

A series of guerrilla incursions, both Communist and non-Communist, were carried out across the Franco-Spanish border in 1945–46. In addition to irregular operations in the countryside, Communist gangs in Spanish towns during the next few years reverted to the old pre-revolutionary Bolshevist tactic of bank robbery to finance their activities. The military chief of Spanish Communism, Enrique Líster, has published an analysis of Communist guerrilla activities in Spain for the years 1944–1949, shown in Table 19.

No great faith should be placed in the precision of these figures, but they give some indication of the degree of armed leftist activity in Spain and also of the relative decline that the Communist portion of the Resistance underwent by 1949. Figures are not available for measuring the relative degree of Communist activity compared with that of the non-Communist resistance groups. Though total support for the non-Communist activists was considerably greater than for the Communists, it may be that the latter bulked disproportionately large in guer-

TABLE 19

Area	1944	1945	1946	1947	1948	1949
Levante and Aragon	78	91	169	217	167	90
Andalusia	150	174	242	288	217	89
Estremadura	102	108	123	172	120	54
Asturias and Santander	109	108	157	200	163	68
Castile	123	124	165	189	122	72
Galicia and Leon	132	178	229	251	194	136
Grand Total	694	783	1,085	1,317	983	509/5,371

SOURCE: *World Marxist Review,* February, 1965, p. 54.

rilla activities because of their ruthlessness.

These operations achieved scant success because much of the population wished for peace and order after the turmoils of the preceding decade, because much of the working classes had become disillusioned with politics, and also because rural society in the northern border regions tends to be quite conservative. The Civil Guard in the countryside and the security police in the cities slowly brought the guerrilla and terrorist squads under control. After 1949–50, their rate of activity dropped off even more sharply, soon vanishing almost altogether.

Since foreign powers were unwilling to take direct action against Franco and most middle-class elements continued passively to accept the regime, the harassing activities of the opposition alone were insufficient to overthrow the government. The surviving minority of Popular Front Cortes members continued to meet abroad infrequently and, backed by their respective *émigré* cliques, quarreled with each other persistently, requiring several reorganizations of the shadow cabinet that was supposed to serve as the Republican Government-in-exile. These maneuvers became less and less meaningful to people inside Spain— even to the active opposition—with each passing year. One decade after the Civil War ended, it was clear that the *émigré* politicians mostly had lost contact with Spanish affairs and no longer wielded significant influence.

If the left-liberal opposition was too weak to remove the regime by itself, then its only immediate hope would be to provoke the defection of elements hitherto influential among and loyal to the Nationalists. The only "Nationalist opposition" to Franco worthy of consideration was that of the monarchists. The end of the Civil War had brought only an institutionalization, not a transformation, of a hybrid non-monarchist dictatorship and, with this, profound disappointment for genuine monarchists. However, the latter had little support in Spanish society and were divided within themselves, like almost all the other Spanish group. The moderates who had formed the "Confederación de Fuerzas Monárquicas" in 1945–46 could not count on the support either of the Army, the greater part of nominal pro-monarchist hangers-on, or, in a showdown, even on the Pretender himself.

Nevertheless, the "Confederación" proposed restoration of a constitutional monarchy with representative guarantees, providing a nucleus of agreement that the moderate left might accept. In 1948, the anti-Communist Socialist leader Indalecio Prieto negotiated with monarchist moderates a tentative agreement—the so-called "Pact of St. Jean de Luz"—to work for the replacement of the present dictatorship by a constitutional monarchy that would convene a democratically elected parliament and permit freedom of trade union organization. These relations were soon broken off, however, because of the opposition of monarchist generals and ultra-conservative supporters. The former resented negotiations with "subversive," "anti-national" elements, and the latter feared even more any kind of deal with the left.

By 1950, Franco had weathered all storms. The entire national committee of the CNT underground had been arrested early in the preceding year, and the Socialists and Communists were effectively repressed. There was a major labor stoppage in Barcelona during the spring of 1951, lasting two or three days and involving up to 300,000 people, but it was largely an economic protest and had no organized political overtones. Except for the nervousness of sectors of the Barcelona police, the regime's response was comparatively mild, for it no longer felt gravely threatened. After almost the entire leadership of the Socialist underground was arrested two years later, the police eased up even more in their harassment, apparently on the theory that the opposition was so thoroughly contained that overly zealous repression might revive the dwindling spirit of rebelliousness. With the economy expanding and the government enjoying the diplomatic and military patronage of the United States, apathy among the opposition became widespread. Even those who were not really apathetic agreed that little was to be accomplished by sticking their necks out under present circumstances.

The spread of apoliticism during the 1950's would have been even more complete had not the country's social and economic structure continued to discriminate rather sharply between "victors" and "vanquished." The Civil War was by no means forgotten since both official propaganda and social and economic perquisites did much to keep it alive. Former Popular Front supporters were still discriminated against in all manner of ways; and the reunification of Spanish society, even among the middle classes, still lay in the future.

During the 1950's, therefore, resistance was largely passive but continued to simmer beneath the surface. Considerable freedom for private dissent existed as long as active conspiracy, public proselytization, or direct action were not resorted to. This permitted a degree of opposition mutterings especially among Catholic and monarchist liberals, who, as "dissident Nationalists," were always treated considerably less harshly than their working class "Red" counterparts. "Gentlemen" political prisoners might sometimes hear the sounds of their working-class Socialist contacts being beaten almost to death in other parts of the prison, while "respectable" middle-class dissidents were treated with relative circumspection.

By the late 1950's, there existed a wide variety of nominal political groups in Spain, most of them semi-clandestine and oriented toward opposition. One observer categorized them as follows:

I. Collaborationist groups who claim to form part of the Opposition:
   A. Opus Dei (middle and upper class, professional and intellectual)
   B. Regular ultra-right wing monarchists (upper class, mostly of the older generation)
   C. Carlists (upper class and Navarrese peasantry)
   D. Ultra-conservative Christian Democrats

II. Right wing of the Opposition:
   A. Dissident Carlists who support D. Juan, the regular Pretender
   B. Unión Española (small group of upper, upper-middle class, moderate pro-monarchist pragmatists)
   C. Group of José Domínguez de Arana (small circle of anti-clerical but otherwise conservative Basque regionalists who support monarchism, rejecting the republicanism of the regular Basque Nationalist Party)
   D. A pleiad of small, moderate, pragmatic upper, upper-middle class groups, among whom may be distinguished:
      1. A faction of conservative ex-Republicans, influential in some professional circles
      2. A faction of pragmatic upper-class monarchists (Valdecasas, Gamero de Castillo)
      3. Other factions of upper-class monarchists, separated from the preceding by personal, clerical, and minor ideological issues

III. Center-right Opposition:
   A. Small pragmatic monarchist faction of Rodríguez Soler
   B. Christian Democrats of José María Gil Robles (potentially influential middle-class group)

IV. Left-center Opposition:
   A. Small pragmatic liberal group of Gregorio Arranza and Miguel Maura
   B. "Partido Social de Acción Democrática" (very small social democratic group led by former Falangist intellectual Dionisio Ridruejo and university professor Enrique Tierno Galvan)
   C. Left-wing Christian Democrats (HOAC, et al.)

V. Leftist Opposition:
   A. Spanish Socialist Party
   B. National Confederation of Labor (or CNT, clandestine Anarcho-Syndicalist federation)
   C. Basque regionalists
   D. Catalan regionalists (includes quite a number of splinter factions)
   E. Spanish Communist Party
   F. Émigré Opposition: Includes *émigré* leadership of:
      1. Republican Government-in-exile
      2. Spanish Socialist Party
      3. National Confederation of Labor
      4. Basque Nationalist Party
      5. Spanish Communist Party

Yet such an analytical listing of the nominal opposition indicates little more than its variety and disunity. Even the potential mass movements of the Left—the Socialists and Anarcho-Syndicalists—had little more than a skeletal cell network organized within Spain. Many of the other opposition factions consisted of little more than a few score intellectual leaders each. All the factors that had created the atmosphere of apoliticism seemed stronger than ever during the late 1950's, and the great majority of Spaniards remained reluctant to become involved with political maneuvers.

The most active and extensive resistance, in the 1960's as in the 1930's, came from the workers of the industrial regions. Yet even this resistance was more concerned with economic than with political matters, and rebel strikers often resisted having their interests identified with abstract political causes unrelated to their most immediate concerns. As explained earlier, the workers tended during the early years of the regime to reject almost altogether the official government trade union system. During the brief period of high hopes of the opposition, in 1945–46, a significant minority of the workers in some regions had affiliated themselves with shadow opposition syndicates. These mostly faded away in the five years that followed. During the 1950's, some of the more idealistic young new middle-class appointees to the posts of syndicate leaders and administrators began to take the interests of the workers more seriously, and the attention of the workers sometimes picked up. It became less common to vote for "Marilyn Monroe" or "Carmen Sevilla" as *enlaces sindicales,* but instead seriously to choose genuine representatives of worker interests—many of them Socialists or Anarchists—at least on the very lowest level, the only one where direct voting was allowed. In turn, as national income mounted and there were greater hopes of focusing interest on economic rather than political matters, the regime itself began to play up the importance of the official trade union system, making syndicalist demagogy and hopes of working-class improvement a major items in its propaganda arsenal.

The climate of economic demagogy that has beset Spain since the 1950's may have distracted attention from political ideology, but it has had the effect of stimulating workers' economic demands. The resultant conflict has been most profound, and the worker opposition most solidly organized, in the mining region of Asturias. Since the rebellion of 1934, the Asturian miners have had a reputation as one of the toughest, most class-conscious worker groups in Spain. Compared with national standards for semi-skilled labor, their wages have always been above average. By the 1950's, however, many of the best Asturian coal seams were becoming exhausted. The majority of the mines were undercapitalized, and the most advanced equipment and safety devices were lacking. Yet, beside the declining mining industry in Spain, there was rising a rapidly growing new heavy metals industry, which by 1962 accounted for 50 percent of the country's iron production. The emergence of major Asturian metallurgy gave one sector of the labor force a new sense of power, while the frustrations of the problematic mining industry left another sector with a heightened sense of grievance. Among the latter, the high accident rate and the slowly improving working conditions increased discontent to a high point by 1962. By April of that year, most mineowners had apparently accepted syndical demands for a daily minimum wage of 160 pesetas ($2.67)—which was 167 percent above the national legal minimum—but a new wage agreement was blocked by red tape in Madrid. A few local syndicate leaders tried to expedite matters but with scant success. Miner activists took the initiative in setting up their own independent shadow unions to develop organizational strength for a strike, spreading into the metallurgical industry as well. The result has been the series of shutdowns that have involved sizable sectors of Asturian industry since 1962. On several occasions, strikes in Asturias have been seconded or paralleled by walkouts among workers at Bilbao and Barcelona. More recently, there have been open labor disputes of one kind or another in almost every industrialized region of Spain. On two occasions, the total number of industrial workers on strike may have reached 100,000 or more. By and large, striking workers have resisted efforts by the Communists and other political groups to employ the strikes for specifically political ends. Their almost exclusively professional and economic orientation has made them all the more difficult for the regime to deal with. Several hundred miners were arrested and sentenced following the first major Asturian strikes, but the solidarity of the worker opposition has become so strong that subsequently many of those arrested have had to be set free for fear of triggering further retaliatory strikes. Sizable wage increases have been won for industrial labor; and, at the beginning of 1963, Franco announced an increase in the national daily minimum wage—exclusive of fringe benefits —to 60 pesetas ($1). The great majority of Spanish labor was already earning more than that, however; and the strikes, effectively organized by industrial labor, have not involved or benefited the nearly one-third of the labor force employed on farms or as domestics outside the syndical system. As previously noted, only very recently has the regime endeavored to improve the latter's lot, obviously to alleviate tensions in such sectors before their frustration gives rise to more radical outbreaks than those of the relatively well-disciplined industrial laborers.

In 1964–65, there also occurred a rash of petty acts of political terrorism in Madrid and several other centers. These consisted mainly of placing at key spots small time bombs primed to go off when the area would be deserted. Such terrorism caused almost no human casualties and seems in large measure to have been the work of the Anarchist youth organization ("Federación Ibérica de Juventudes Libertarias"), operating from southwestern France. Within a year or so, most of the terrorists were rounded up.

Since Franco passed his seventieth birthday, there has been some slight tendency for previously apathetic middle-class elements to take more serious thought for the political future. A quarter-century of peace and quiet, together with fifteen years of relative economic well-being, has to some degree dulled the caste fear that so long sustained Franco's system of divide and rule. In the 1960's, it has become increasingly difficult to justify dictatorship by fanning memories of the Civil War of the previous epoch. Though all key elements of the regime (and the loose Nationalist confederation of political factions) remain more or less faithful to Franco, there is increasing reluctance to go all out in upholding the government, or to display violent hostility toward the opposition. The regime has no longer been able to muster the psychological support for the degree of repression that would have seemed natural twenty years earlier.

This climate of laxity made it possible for a mob of nearly one thousand miners to sack a local police headquarters in the Asturian town of Mieres on the evening of March 12, 1965. Official spokesmen went through their customary gesture of blaming this on "Communists," but much more notable was the fact that the Ministry of the Interior did not respond with the sort of reprisal that in early years would have been inevitable. Student disorders at the Universities of Madrid and Barcelona against the government-appointed student syndicate brought similar gestures of hesitation and uncertainty from the Ministry of Education.

By the end of 1965, the Cortes approved revision of Article 222 of the Spanish Penal Code to exclude prosecution of strikers engaged purely in labor disputes without direct political involvement. After thirty years of national syndicalism, the "right to strike" had at last been conceded. A minority of 35 appointed deputies caused a small sensation by voting against the bill on the grounds that "it did not go far enough." The state's official political organ, *Arriba*, some time earlier had spoken of the greater need for "dialogue" between differing viewpoints, essential to any "true democracy."

It cannot be said that the passage of time and the increasing leniency of the dictatorship have resulted in greater unity or clearer planning among the kaleidoscope of opposition cliques.

For the most part, they remain as fractionalized—and frequently as vague in their thinking—as ever. Yet such was the case in Italy in 1942, where the new configuration of representative government did not emerge until some years after the dictatorship had been overthrown. If the inchoate character of the Spanish opposition inspires no confidence about the country's future after the passing of the Franco regime, it would be rash to predict in advance the nature or outcome of Spain's response to its impending political dilemma.

Bibliography

The best one-volume account of modern Spanish history is Raymond Carr, *Spain 1808–1939* (Oxford, 1966). Carlos Seco Serrano's *La época contemporánea,* the sixth volume of the Instituto Gallach's *Historia de España* (Barcelona, 1962), provides a useful survey of twentieth-century Spain. On the background of the Second Republic, see Gerald Brenan, *The Spanish Labyrinth* (London, 1943) and Carlos M. Rama, *La crisis española del siglo XX* (Mexico City, 1960). The best general treatment of Spain in the 1930's is Gabriel Jackson, *The Spanish Republic and the Civil War, 1931–1939* (Princeton, 1965). Two helpful accounts by conservatives that offer a great deal of factual detail are José Pla, *Historia de la segunda República española* (Barcelona, 1940–41), 4 vols., and Joaquín Arrarás, *Historia de la segunda República española* (Madrid, 1958, 1964), of which the two volumes thus far completed extend only to the close of 1934. The best surveys of the Civil War are Hugh Thomas, *The Spanish Civil War* (New York, 1961) and Pierre Broué and Emile Témime, *La Révolution et la guerre d'Espagne* (Paris, 1961).

There are numerous biographies of Franco, none of them objective. Perhaps the least inadequate is Claude Martin, *Franco, soldat et Chef d'Etat* (Paris, 1959). The first official biography was Joaquín Arrarás, *Franco* (San Sebastián, 1937), followed by at least fifteen other laudatory sketches written by supporters of the regime. Of these, the two most useful are Fernando de Valdesoto, *Francisco Franco* (Madrid, 1943) and Luis Galinsoga and Lt. Gen. Francisco Franco Salgado-Araujo, *Centinela de Occidente* (Barcelona, 1956). The most sustained biographical denunciation is Luis Ramírez (pseud.), *Francisco Franco (Historia de un mesianismo)* (Paris, 1965).

The official history of the Nationalist movement is Joaquín Arrarás, ed., *Historia de la Cruzada española* (Madrid, 1940), 8 vols. Military aspects are treated in Manuel Aznar, *Historia militar de la guerra de España* (Madrid, 1940); Lt. Col. Luis María de Lojendio, *Operaciones militares de la guerra de España 1936–1939* (Barcelona, 1940); *Guerra de liberación nacional* (Zaragoza, 1961); and in a special number of the Servicio Histórico Militar's *Revista de Historia Militar* (No. 17, 1965). On the role of the military in general, see Stanley G. Payne, *Politics and the Military in Modern Spain* (Stanford, 1967).

The aspect of the Franco regime that has attracted the greatest amount of study is foreign relations. Manfred Merkes, *Die deutsche Politik gegenüber dem spanischen Bürgerkrieg 1936–1939* (Bonn, 1961), Glenn T. Harper, *German Economic Policy in Spain during the Spanish Civil War, 1936–1939* (The Hague, 1965), and Donald S. Detwiler, *Hitler, Franco und Gibraltar: Die Frage des spanischen Eintritts in den Zweiten Weltkrieg* (Wiesbaden, 1962) are published doctoral dissertations. Among the unpublished dissertations are Robert A. Friedlander, "The July 1936 Military Rebellion in Spain" (Northwestern, 1963), which studies both the domestic and international dimensions of the beginning of the Nationalist movement; Albert C. Horton, "Germany and the Spanish Civil War" (Columbia, 1966); Robert H. Whealey, "German-Spanish Relations January–August 1939" (Michigan, 1963); and Charles R. Halstead, "Spain, the Powers and the Second World War" (Virginia, 1962). Herbert Feis, *The*

Spanish Story (New York, 1948) provides an objective account of the main aspects of Franco's relations with the Western allies during the war. The principal apologium for Franco's wartime diplomacy is José María Doussinague, *España tenía razón (1939-1945)* (Madrid, 1950), while E.-N. Dzelepy, *Franco, Hitler et les Alliés* (Brussels, 1961), is a thoroughly hostile critique. On the military agreement with the United States, there are Theodore J. Lowi, "Bases in Spain," in Harold Stein, ed., *American Civil-Military Decisions* (Birmingham, Ala.), pp. 667–700, and an unpublished dissertation by Robert Wozniecki, "Las Bases Conjuntas Hispano-Americanas, 1951–1960" (University of Madrid, 1960).

To this date, very little memoir literature has come out of the regime. The only volumes worth noting are Ramón Serrano Súñer, *Entre Hendaya y Gibraltar* (Mexico City, 1945) and Ramón Garriga, *Las relaciones secretas entre Franco y Hitler* (Buenos Aires, 1965), both of which deal with foreign affairs; Lt. Gen. Alfredo Kindelán, *Mis cuadernos de guerra 1936–1939* (Madrid, 1945) and Juan Antonio Ansaldo, *¿Para qué . . . ? (De Alfonso XIII a Juan III)* (Buenos Aires, 1954), on military matters and monarchist politics; and for domestic politics, Dionisio Ridruejo, *Escrito en España* (Buenos Aires, 1962) and Alfona Peña Boeuf, *Memorias de un ingeniero político* (Madrid, 1954). The changes in the regime's position may be traced in the collected speeches of Franco and some of his leading ministers, such as Serrano Súñer, Raimundo Fernández Cuesta and José Luis de Arrese, which have been published periodically since 1939.

The nominal structure of the regime and its achievements are set forth in *El Nuevo Estado español 1936–1963* (Madrid, 1963), 2 vols. For a sophisticated effort to establish a legal basis for dictatorship, see Pascual Marín Pérez, *El Caudillaje español* (Madrid, 1960). Stanley G. Payne, *Falange* (Stanford,

1961) treats Franco's official political movement and William G. Ebenstein, *Church and State in Franco Spain* (Princeton, 1960) analyzes another important dimension of public affairs. Though mainly concerned with politics and foreign relations, Arthur S. Whitaker's *Spain and Defense of the West* (New York, 1961) provides a sound general study of Spanish problems as of 1960. Much of Elena de la Souchère, *An Explanation of Spain* (New York, 1964), is devoted to a critical and somewhat exaggerated survey of the regime. Among the least misleading early journalist accounts were Emmett J. Hughes, *Report from Spain* (New York, 1947) and Charles S. Foltz, *The Masquerade in Spain* (Boston, 1948). The best recent treatments by newspapermen are Jean Créac'h, *Le Coeur et l'épée* (Paris, 1959) and Benjamin Welles, *Spain, the Gentle Anarchy* (New York, 1965).

Perhaps the most prolific economist in Franco's Spain has been Higinio París Eguilaz. Basic changes in the political and economic policies of the regime are reflected in the titles of two of his books, *El Estado y la economía política totalitaria* (Burgos, 1938) and *El Plan económico en la sociedad libre: Perspectivas de un Plan en España* (Madrid, 1947). Other studies by París Eguilaz include *España en la economía mundial* (Madrid, 1947), *Diez años de política económica en España 1939–1949* (Madrid, 1949), *Inversiones y desarrollo económico en España* (Madrid, 1956), *Factores del desarrollo económico español* (Madrid, 1957) and *Renta nacional, inversión y consumo en España 1939–1959* (Madrid, 1960).

The principal study of the contemporary Spanish economy is Ramón Tamames, *Estructura económica de España* (Madrid, 1960). There are a number of useful economic geographies of Spain, such as Joaquín Bosque Maurel, *Geografía económica de España* (Barcelona, 1960), Francisco Cortada Reus, *Geografía económica de España* (Barcelona, 1946), and Manuel Fuentes Irurozqui, *Viaje a través de la España económica* (Madrid, 1948). Serious studies of aspects or periods of the economy under

Franco include Miguel Capella, *La autarquía económica en España* (Madrid, 1945), John H. Kemler, *The Struggle for Wolfram in the Iberian Peninsula June 1942–June 1944* (Chicago, 1949), Heinrich Klaus, *Strukturwandlungen und Nachkriegsprobleme der Wirtschaft Spaniens* (Kiel, 1954), Jacques Milleron, *Etude sur l'économie espagnole* (Rabat, 1955), E. Fuentes Quintana and J. Fuentes Velarde, *Política económica* (Madrid, 1957), Banco Urquijo, *Stabilization Policy in Spain 1959–1961* (Madrid, 1961), Antonio Robert, *A Report on the Spanish Economy and European Integration* (Madrid, 1960), International Bank, *Economic Development of Spain* (Baltimore, 1963) and Manuel Tuñón de Lara, *Panorama actual de la economía española* (Paris, 1962). The two principal studies of the problem of monopoly are Ramón Tamames, *La lucha contra los monopolios en España* (Madrid, 1959) and Fermín de la Sierra, *La concentración en las industrias básicas españolas* (Madrid, 1953).

In the analysis of social change, attention should be drawn to the work of the sociologists Juan J. Linz and Amando de Miguel. In addition to their major study, *El empresario español como factor humano en el desarrollo económico* (Madrid, 1965), they have made a useful analysis of regional social differences, "Within-Nation Differences and Comparisons: The Eight Spains," in Richard L. Merritt and Stein Rokkan, eds., *Comparing Nations* (New Haven, 1966), pp. 267–318.

For an analysis of the Spanish Catholic Church in recent years see Pierre Jobit, *L'Eglise d'Espagne a l'heure du Concile* (Paris, 1965). Jacques Delpech, *The Oppression of Protestants in Spain* (Boston, 1955), is a helpful introduction to the problems of Spanish Protestantism.

On the problem of internal and external emigration, there are Vicente Borregón Ribes, *La emigración española a América* (Vigo, 1952), Joaquim Maluquer i Sostres, *L'Assimilation des immigrés en Catalogne* (Geneva, 1963), and Francesco Candel, *Els altres catalans* (Barcelona, 1964).

For the Spanish novel of the 1940's and 1950's, see Juan Luis Alborg, *Hora actual de la novela española* (Madrid, 1958). Eduardo Comín Colomer, *La República en el exilio* (Barcelona, 1957), provides detailed treatment of the exiled opposition, but is extremely biased and sometimes inaccurate. For an account by a Syndicalist of the political problems of the émigrés, see Fidel Miró, *¿Y España cuándo?* (Mexico City, 1959). Juan García Durán, *Por la libertad* (Mexico City, 1956), gives an interesting autobiographical account of the struggles of the domestic opposition. Scores of newspapers and periodicals have been published by political exiles. Two of the best and longest lived are based in New York: *Ibérica* (in English) and *España Libre*. The most acute Spanish leftist journal published in Europe is *Cuadernos de Ruedo Ibérico* (Paris, 1965–   ).

Index